Serene Reflection Meditation
by
Rev. Master
P.T.N.H. Jiyu-Kennett
and

Members of the
Order of Buddhist Contemplatives

Shasta Abbey, Mt. Shasta, California

Eighth edition revised—2016

Originally published in 1974 as *Zen Meditation*, with revised second and third editions in 1976 and 1980. The fourth revised edition was published in England in 1987 as Serene Reflection Meditation. The fifth revised edition was published in 1989 and the sixth revised edition in 1996. The seventh edition was put on the internet. Copyright of each of the articles that appear herein belongs to its respective author. Enquiries regarding reprints or quotations may be directed to the individual authors or to the publisher, who will pass them on.

Shasta Abbey
3724 Summit Drive
Mt. Shasta, California 96067-9102
(530) 926-4208

Poem (opposite Contents page):
based upon the first four sections of chapter VIII
of the Udana Scripture.

Photograph on front cover is of a statue of
the Buddha on the Shasta Abbey grounds.

ISBN 978-0-930066-28-4

In gratitude to Rev. Master Jiyu-Kennett
for showing us the Way

O monks, there is an Unborn,
Undying, Uncreated, Unformed;
Were It not, there could be no end
to birth, decay, disease, and death.

Hard It is to find,
the Truth no easy thing to know;
Craving is pierced by one who seeth,
no self remains, no earthly woes;
for him: eternal life, serene repose.

Contents

Rules for Meditation

[This scripture was written by Great Master Dogen, the founder of the Serene Reflection Meditation tradition in Japan. It is studied in great detail and recited daily at mid-day service in churches and monasteries of the Serene Reflection Meditation tradition.][1]

Why are training and enlightenment differentiated since the Truth is universal? Why study the means of attaining it since the supreme teaching is free? Since Truth is seen to be clearly apart from that which is unclean, why cling to a means of cleansing it? Since Truth is not separate from training, training is unnecessary— the separation will be as that between heaven and earth if even the slightest gap exists FOR, WHEN THE OPPOSITES ARISE, THE BUDDHA MIND IS LOST. However much you may be proud of your understanding, however much you may be enlightened, whatever your attainment of wisdom and supernatural power, your finding of the way to mind illumination, your power to touch heaven and to enter into enlightenment, when the opposites arise you have almost lost the way to salvation. Although the Buddha had great wisdom at birth, He sat in training for six years; although Bodhidharma Transmitted the Buddha Mind, we still hear the echoes of his nine years facing a wall. The Ancestors were very diligent and there is no reason why we people of the present day cannot understand. All you have to do is cease from erudition, withdraw within and reflect upon yourself. Should you be able to cast off body and mind naturally, the Buddha Mind will immediately manifest itself; if you want to find it quickly, you must start at once.

You should meditate in a quiet room, eat and drink moderately, cut all ties, give up everything, think of neither good nor evil, consider neither right nor wrong. Control mind function, will, consciousness, memory, perception and understanding; you must not strive thus to become Buddha. Cling to neither sitting nor lying down. When meditating, do not wear tight clothing. Rest the left hand in the palm of the right hand with the thumbs touching lightly; sit upright, leaning neither to left nor right, backwards nor forwards.

1

The ears must be in line with the shoulders and the nose in line with the navel; the tongue must be held lightly against the back of the top teeth with the lips and teeth closed. Keep the eyes open, breathe in quickly, settle the body comfortably and breathe out sharply. Sway the body left and right then sit steadily, neither trying to think nor trying not to think; just sitting, with no deliberate thought, is the important aspect of serene reflection meditation.

This type of meditation is not something that is done in stages; it is simply the lawful gateway to carefree peace. To train and enlighten ourselves is to become thoroughly wise; the koan appears *naturally* in daily life. If you become thus utterly free you will be as the water wherein the dragon dwells or as the mountain whereon the tiger roams. Understand clearly that the Truth appears naturally and then your mind will be free from doubts and vacillation. When you wish to arise from meditation, sway the body gently from side to side and arise quietly; the body must make no violent movement; I myself have seen that the ability to die whilst sitting and standing, which transcends both peasant and sage, is obtained through the power of serene reflection meditation. It is no more possible to understand natural activity with the judgemental mind than it is possible to understand the signs of enlightenment; nor is it possible to understand training and enlightenment by supernatural means; such understanding is outside the realm of speech and vision, such Truth is beyond personal opinions. Do not discuss the wise and the ignorant, there is only one thing—to train hard for this is true enlightenment; training and enlightenment are naturally undefiled; to live in this way is the same as to live an ordinary daily life. The Buddha Seal has been preserved by both the Buddhas in the present world and by those in the world of the Indian and Chinese Ancestors, they are thus always spreading the Truth—*all* activity is permeated with pure meditation—the means of training are thousandfold but pure meditation must be done. It is futile to travel to other dusty countries thus forsaking your own seat; if your first step is false, you will immediately stumble. Already you are in possession of the vital attributes of a human being—do not waste time with this and that—*you* can possess the authority of Buddha. Of what use is it to merely enjoy this fleeting world? This body is as transient as dew on the grass, life passes as swiftly as a flash of lightning, quickly the body passes away, in a moment life is gone. O sincere trainees, do not doubt the true dragon, do not spend so much time in rubbing only a part of the elephant; look *inwards* and advance directly along the road that leads to the Mind, respect those who have reached the goal of goallessness, become one with the wisdom of the Buddhas, *Transmit* the wisdom of the Ancestors. If you do these things for some time you will become as herein described and then the Treasure House will open naturally and you will enjoy it fully.

Note

1. We have removed the sections that describe meditation in cross-legged positions from the *Rules for Meditation*. Rev. Master Jiyu-Kennett explains: "We found that this type of sitting, when practiced by people who sat alone, injured too many legs and backs. If there are persons who would really like to learn this method we can show it to them but we are keeping it out of the *Rules for Meditation* from here on so that people do not suffer from the idea that this is the only way to go; there are other methods and they are just as effective and a lot safer for western people."

Commentary on Dogen's "Rules for Meditation"

Rev. Master Jiyu-Kennett

If you wish to harmonise body and mind it is <u>absolutely impera-tive</u> that you study the Rules for Meditation in <u>detail</u>. <u>First, and foremost, keep your eyes open</u>—otherwise you can get into a trance state in which you can accidentally die.

<u>Second</u>, control mind function, will, consciousness, memory, per-ception and understanding—if any one of these is allowed to pre-dominate the balance and rhythm of the meditation will be upset and you will get nowhere. Be alert enough so that, whenever one or the other of these conditions begins to appear, you do not become attached to it so that you follow it to the detriment of the meditation; awareness is the key-word here.

<u>Third</u>, it does not <u>matter</u> whether you are sitting or lying down al-though the latter should only be used <u>constantly</u> if you are sick; laziness must be guarded against at all times; right effort is <u>always</u> required.

<u>Fourth</u>, do not worry about thoughts coming and going; just do <u>not</u> grab at them and do <u>not</u> push them away; watch them flow by natu-rally and do not be concerned with or interested in them.

<u>Fifth</u>, take two or three deep breaths when you <u>start</u> to meditate and then allow the breathing to become natural; do <u>not</u> try to make it dif-ferent from what is <u>natural breathing for you</u>. Correct breathing is absolutely essential if one would meditate properly and this is only achieved if the meditator knows how to <u>follow</u> the breath properly.

Reprinted from Rev. Roshi Jiyu-Kennett's *How to Grow a Lotus Blossom or How a Zen Buddhist Prepares for Death* (Mt. Shasta, California: Shasta Abbey Press, 1977), pp. 186–190.

If one would follow the breath properly one must, as it states at the beginning of the *Rules for Meditation*, take two or three good breaths and then remain sitting quietly, allowing the breath to be perfectly natural. But not nearly enough has been said about these two or three 'good breaths' because it is not the depth of the breath but the path it takes that is absolutely essential to proper meditation.

Because of the mistakes made with regard to the last mentioned this commentary is chiefly concerned with <u>how</u> to take those two or three deep breaths.

Shakyamuni Buddha, after trying many harsh disciplines, and finding them useless, decided to try the method of breathing He had used as a child of seven. He was <u>immediately</u> successful in His attempts to reach enlightenment; He succeeded <u>that very same night</u>. Every small child knows how to meditate properly; it is only after we have "educated" it that its body and mind become separated and this was just as true of Shakyamuni Buddha as it is of us. This separation of body and mind can be precipitated by many things <u>besides</u> "education"; <u>anything</u>, in fact, that instils greed for worldly gain through competitiveness (the main cause of the disharmony of body and mind and its resulting tensions which ultimately lead to ill-health). Constantly quarrelling parents, or parents that do not make a secure home for their children, can cause the separation a lot earlier than the age of seven. This being so, he who would meditate properly must set up the breathing pattern that he used as a child. Here is how it is done.

The breath originates in the hara, an area roughly triangular in shape with its base in the area of the navel and its apex at the base of the sternum, the sides roughly corresponding to the sides of the rib cage. One should not count breaths when meditating; one should <u>follow the course</u> that the breath takes. Most people breathe without thinking about it but the meditator must <u>consciously</u>, at the <u>beginning</u> of each meditation, as well as at any time he <u>loses</u> his awareness during that meditation, <u>follow one or two</u> breaths thus:– Imagine, when taking these breaths, that at inhalation the breath starts at the base of the spine, continues up the spine and does not cease to move until it reaches the crown of the head which is the moment at which exhalation begins. The breath then continues down the front of the body during exhalation to the pubic area where inhalation takes over at the base of the spine. Thus the breath seems to travel in a circle, inhalation up the back of the body and exhalation down the front; it is <u>absolutely vital</u> that it travels up the spine and down the sternum.

This circular breathing is called "the turning of the Wheel of the Law"— and there is good reason for the name! If you set this back-flowing wheel, as it were, in motion during these two or three breaths then the whole pattern for meditation is correctly set and the breath will flow clearly, cleanly, and correctly and the meditation will be full and adequate.

There are some other things of importance here: in <u>meditation</u> this following of the breath is done consciously <u>two or three times</u> so that the breathing pattern may be established both physically and psychologically and then it must be <u>left behind</u> and the breathing allowed to settle <u>naturally</u> into the rhythm that is right for the individual. Above all, <u>do not</u> try to follow the breath in this way during the entire meditation. That pattern should only be set up again if the mind wanders much or if the mind falls out of meditation; then two or three more breaths should be taken in the same way and the pattern again set up.

When one finds that this type of breathing is so natural that it is second-nature to him he will notice that there are tiny fractions of time, called the 'apertures' in the breath, between inhalation and exhalation. If he has been able to learn how <u>not</u> to be distracted by his thoughts he will be still enough to hear the still, small voice, the voice of the Lord of the House,[1] during these tiny intervals: it is by means of listening to the Lord in these small intervals that body and mind once again enter into harmony.

When a person has become good at meditating in this way, which is nothing other than sitting quietly as the *Rules for Meditation* state, he will find that he can hear the still, small voice in other places. When he is good at this the still, small voice, his true nature, will take over from the voice of his egocentric ego—the roles that these two have played since the meditator suffered the disharmony of body and mind as a child will be reversed and then genuine spiritual progress is possible. The Christians call this state 'having conversations with God'; the Buddhist calls it the harmonisation of body and mind—it is explained elaborately in the Goi theory of Tozan.[2] The *Sandokai*[3] should be studied deeply in connection with this.

Understand that <u>none</u> of the above can take place until the <u>involvement</u> in the <u>noise</u> of the human brain dies down; a person who is constantly chasing after his own thoughts and getting involved with them will be too busy to <u>hear</u> the Lord of the House!

Notes

1. See Great Master Keizan's "Denkoroku" ("The Transmission of the Light"), chapters 1, 2 and 7 in *Zen is Eternal Life* by Roshi P.T.N.H. Jiyu-Kennett, 3rd ed. rev. (Mt. Shasta, California: Shasta Abbey Press, 1987).
2. The teaching of the Five Ranks by Great Master Tozan Ryokai, the founder of the Serene Reflection Meditation tradition in China, describes the relationship of the Eternal and the Apparent.
3. A Scripture by Great Master Sekito Kisen that describes the harmonisation of the "all is one" with the "all is different"; a translation of it is to be found in *The Liturgy of the Order of Buddhist Contemplatives for the Laity*, comp. Rev. Master P.T.N.H. Jiyu-Kennett, M.O.B.C., 2nd ed. rev. (Mt. Shasta, California: Shasta Abbey Press, 1990), pp. 59–61.

How to Sit

Rev. Master Jiyu-Kennett

When sitting, one should take care that one's spine follows the <u>natural</u> curvature of a <u>healthy</u> spine, as seen in any good medical book, as much as possible. It is very important for a person learning to sit to get this right. What happens with the feet is not important; what happens to one's spine is of the utmost importance. If the spine is not correct for the individual concerned, stiffness, pain and perhaps even hallucinations may result. The weight of the body is carried easily by the lower back muscles if this position is correct; one does tend, however, to develop something of a bulge in the front, popularly called a "Zazen pot." This cannot be helped and should not be worried about. It sometimes happens that a person may have had a back injury of some sort during his or her earlier years and this may make sitting with a spine <u>exactly</u> right extraordinarily difficult. You should know that what we are attempting to do is to find the place where a person can sit <u>best</u> so as to have the very best results possible.

One never sits completely back upon the cushion or chair. When sitting on the floor, only the tip of the base of the spine should actually be on the cushion itself so that there is a slight slope from the buttocks, just seated on the edge of the cushion, to the floor where the knees rest comfortably. This posture prevents anything from pressing upon the thighs which may restrict the blood flow. If one sits fully upon the cushion, without allowing this free space for the thighs, it will be impossible to move from the cushion without considerable pain at a later date. The head should feel naturally comfortable and weightless upon the shoulders, with the ears in line with the latter and the nose in line with the navel. No two people are exactly the same physically so it is very important to experiment carefully for yourself so that you can be certain that you have found the right place for your head

This article is taken from a lecture by Rev. Master Jiyu-Kennett.

and the right place for your feet. If your ears are not <u>exactly</u> in line with your shoulders as a result of a back injury of some sort, do <u>not</u> feel that you cannot meditate. Find that place in which you are most comfortable, i.e. the place where you are most weightless, and commence your meditation in that position. One sways one's body from left to right, after the correct sitting position has been achieved, starting with large sways and ending with smaller and smaller ones; one can do circular swaying instead of this if one wishes. These types of movement enable a person to find the best position of rest for him or her as an individual; the place at which all his or her weight seems to drop straight down the spine and into the cushion or onto the chair.

The hands must not be pushed together but held in the lap with the thumbs lightly touching the ends of each other as in the illustration [on page 20]. A left-handed person places the right hand over the left, and a right-handed person the left hand over the right, for the following reason:– one side of the body is always slightly more active than the other, usually the side that one uses most, therefore, during seated meditation, one puts the hand of the less active side over the hand of the more active one since it is believed that this helps to equate the unevenness of the body's activity.

No one should ever close their eyes completely. They should be lowered so that they rest upon a spot on the floor that the meditator can see comfortably. No two people are ever comfortable at <u>exactly</u> the same distance of focus, therefore, although it is customary to say that it is best to allow the eyes to rest upon the floor at a distance of about one metre, it should be understood that this is not a hard and fast rule. Neither a short-sighted nor a long-sighted person could achieve this. One does not sit in meditation to do that which is unnatural for oneself, therefore, if it is normal for a person to wear spectacles, he should continue to do so whilst meditating; he should not remove them. The natural inheritance and right of all of us is to know our True Selves, that is, to be peaceful and at one with the Eternal; in order to achieve this we must not do something that is <u>unnatural</u> for <u>us</u>, as individuals, simply because meditation instructions that have been written for the perfect body say that we should.

Question:– I am near-sighted, should I still wear my spectacles?

Answer:– As I have just said, it is important that your eyes shall be able to focus <u>normally</u> and <u>naturally</u> on a spot that is comfortable. If a person is facing a wall which is, at most, six feet or so away from him, and happens to be near-sighted, he may not <u>need</u> to wear his spectacles; if he is far-sighted he probably <u>will</u> need them.

Question:– What should I look at?

Answer:– It is important to do much the same thing with the eyes that one does with one's mind. One must neither try to see anything specific, such as the patterns on the wall or floor, nor try to make such things blurry and indistinct. One should simply keep the eyes downcast and in focus. One keeps one's eyes open so as to be able to stay awake and alert. A person is not <u>trying</u> to see and, at the same time, he is not trying not to see.

It is important to breathe through the nose and not through the mouth. This is achieved quite simply by keeping the mouth shut and nothing more. It is not a hard, tight shutting that may cause the teeth to grind; it is just a simple, comfortable closing of the mouth.

When breathing, a person must not do anything that is unnatural. There are many and varied forms of so-called meditation, all of which give varying degrees of spiritual comfort. There is no form that gives greater spiritual comfort, and deeper understanding and awareness, than serene reflection meditation as far as I am concerned; however, these benefits can only be achieved if one breathes naturally. It is important to synchronise one's breathing with the natural state of one's own body. If the breathing is rough, i.e. strained or made unusual by the individual concerned, there can be no harmonisation whatsoever of body and mind. Some of us breathe more quickly than others, others more slowly. Each person must breathe in his or her own normal, natural rhythm so that no unusual stresses or strains are caused. Again, the accent is on <u>not</u> being unnatural.

One must not deliberately try to think nor deliberately try not to think. Thoughts come and go in our heads and we can either play with them or just sit there and allow them to pass. Too many of us allow ourselves to be hijacked by our thoughts whilst some try to deliberately push them away; both of these activities are completely incorrect. The Japanese distinguish between deliberate thought and natural thought. There is <u>absolutely nothing wrong</u> with natural thought. Because our ears are not plugged up during meditation, it is normal for us to hear cars passing on the roads and birds singing; because our eyes are not closed, it is only reasonable that we will notice patterns on the carpet, floor or wall: these things will only disturb us if we permit ourselves to discuss them in our own minds. If one merely notices that a car is going by there will be no problem however, if one notices that a car is going by and becomes annoyed or pleased about it, then meditation has already ceased. All that is required in meditation is that one sit with a positive attitude of mind, knowing that, if one does so, one will indeed find the True Buddha within oneself.

I have often used the example of sitting under a bridge to illustrate the above. One sits beneath a bridge across which traffic is travelling in both directions. One does not climb upon the bridge to hitch a ride in one of the cars, nor does one chase after them; one also makes no attempt to push the cars off the bridge. One cannot ignore that the cars are there; one does not have to be bothered by them. If a person does get caught by his or her thoughts which, in the beginning, is quite likely, it is important not to worry about it. One merely accepts the fact that one was caught and continues to sit, without worrying about the fact that one was caught or being guilty about it. No matter what one does, one cannot <u>change</u> the fact that one was caught and, if one worries about it, one just does not become peaceful enough to return to meditation. One should avoid guilt at all costs concerning this; there is nothing so destructive as guilt in this regard.

When the meditation is over, one sways the body from side to side or in a circular motion, exactly as one did at the beginning, except that one commences with small sways and ends with large ones.

It is important not to wear anything that is either tight or constricting. It is equally important to dress adequately so that one is neither too hot nor too cold. Great Master Dogen, when speaking of excesses, i.e. too much warmth, too much clothing, too much food, not enough warmth, not enough clothing, not enough food, makes the following comment: "Six parts of a full stomach support the man, the other two support his doctor." One must make sure that one is adequately fed and clothed, with just the right amount of rest, and thereafter not indulge oneself. Great Master Dogen gives a very important warning concerning what he calls the three lacks, i.e. lack of sleep, lack of food and lack of warmth. Unless these three are exactly right, neither too much nor too little of any, the harmonisation of body and mind is impossible.

Question:− What happens if a person is halfway through a meditation period and cannot continue to hold the same sitting position?

Answer:− It is advisable to move and not worry about doing so. Seated meditation is not an endurance test. If a person feels that he or she cannot maintain the meditation position, there is nothing whatsoever wrong with changing it. Should it become necessary to move, it is very important to remember that the spine shall again be correctly aligned. It is also important to discipline oneself to a certain extent. I have always maintained that a person who feels that he can sit for ten minutes should push himself to sit for twelve minutes and that, when he is able to sit for twelve minutes, he should push himself to sit for fourteen minutes. He should continue in this way until he can maintain the same position during the full forty-five-minute sitting period without discomfort. By such means the body is disciplined gently and naturally whilst recognising that it has rights. If it is not done in this way, sitting may become something that is dreaded; I know of nothing worse than this.

Question:− What about fidgeting?

Answer:− If a person wishes to progress in meditation, it is very important for him or her to learn to sit <u>still</u>. Fidgeting, if the body is not uncomfortable, is a sign of a person's dislike of discipline and is a measure of the ego that is, as yet, unconverted. The debate of the opposites in our minds is not always as clearcut as we think, and the urge to fidget is sometimes a reaction to our unwillingness to do something about ourselves. If a person finds himself suffering from the urge to fidget, he should take two or three deep breaths and again realign his body since he will probably have become tense and stiff in the shoulders.

If we were all short, fat, thin or tall, had exactly the same eyesight or were in exactly the same state of health, it would be extraordinarily easy to teach meditation. However, each one of us is totally different, and this means that it is impossible to write a chapter on the mode of physical sitting necessary for meditation which will be exactly the same for everyone. It is important for a person to have himself or herself checked carefully by a competent teacher to find what is exactly the right position for him or her as an individual. Too many people try to keep the letter of the physical *Rules for Meditation* without realising that the purpose of them is to help them learn to meditate, not to cause them physical pain and unnatural discomfort.

Serene Reflection

Rev. Master Koten Benson

The term *serene reflection* has been in general use since the time of Great Master Wanshi Shokaku, 1091–1157,[1] to describe the original meditation practice of the Ch'an (Zen) tradition,[2] in contrast to the *introspecting the koan* (C: *k'ang hua*; J: *kanna-zen*) method that was then becoming popular through the teaching of the master Daie, 1089 –1163.[3]

"Serene reflection" is a translation of two Chinese characters, *mo* (J: *moku*) and *chao* (J: *sho*). A study of these characters and the levels of meaning within them may be of help to us in understanding more about our practice. I am by no means an expert in the Chinese language so I have made use of several dictionaries, books of character analysis and commentaries on the term itself to put together this article and ask forgiveness for its shortcomings.

The first character, *mo*, has an element in it that means black or darkness, making the whole character signify "dark, secret, silent, serene, profound" and also "to close the lips, to become silent".

The second character, *chao*, has as element meaning "the brightness of the sun". The whole character translates as "to reflect light, to shine on, to illume or enlighten", as well as "to reflect upon, to look upon, to have insight into".

The whole term thus becomes "serene reflection", "silent illumination"[4] or "luminescent darkness".[5] In the very description of our practice we have the 'light in darkness—darkness in light' spoken of in the works of the great masters of our tradition.[6]

We can also see in this the origin of the references to the reflection of the moon in water. As the water of the spirit within us becomes still, clean and bright through meditation, so does the reflection of the "moon", of the Eternal, become clear and True. There is more

Reprinted from *The Journal of the Order of Buddhist Comtemplatives*, vol. 4, no. 1: 33 – 35.

than "stillness" in this, more than mere quietism. The water must be clear and bright and clean or there will only be the false "stillness" of stagnation, a dirty pool in which the moon's reflection will be dim and shallow. This is why we are warned about the consequences of clinging to blissful states and urged to maintain a bright mind while meditating—the importance of the 'stillness within activity and activity within stillness'.

Another important point in the characters is that there is no "thing" that can be grasped as the source of the light nor a "thing" that reflects the shining. Neither is the darkness or silence a "thing" that can be grasped. This is because in the face-to-face encounter with the Eternal of meditation there is no separate self, just the serene, profound, illuminating light.

Dogen says it better than I:

> Lament impurity.
> Within the silent waters of the heart
> Dwells the moon, the lonely waves—
> Brightness everywhere.[7]

Notes

1. Hung Chih Cheng Chueh, disciple of Tanka Shijun, author of *Mo Chao Ming* (*Notes on Serene Reflection*).
2. Chang, *The Practice of Zen*, pp. 66–69.
3. Ta Hui Tsung Kao (J: Daie Soko).
4. Another translation of *mo chao*.
5. See Rev. Master P.T.N.H. Jiyu-Kennett, M.O.B.C., *How to Grow a Lotus Blossom or How a Zen Buddhist Prepares for Death*, 2nd ed. rev. (Mount Shasta, California: Shasta Abbey, 1993), p. 165.
6. See *Hsin Hsin Ming* (*Faith in Mind*) by Kanchi Sosan; *Ts'an T'ung Ch'i* (*Sandokai*) by Sekito Kisen; *Pao Ching San Mei Ko* (*The Most Excellent Mirror–Samadhi*) by Tozan Ryokai; *Mo Chao Ming (Notes on Serene Reflection)* by Wanshi Shokaku; "Ko Myo" ("Divine Light"), chapter 13 of *Shobogenzo* by Dogen; *Komyozo-Zanmai* (*Samadhi of the Treasury of the Radiant Light*) by Koun Ejo and many other works in various translations.

7. See *The Story of Rev. Dogen*, translated from the Japanese by Rev. P.T.N.H. Jiyu-Kennett.

Bibliography

1. Chang, Garma C.C. *The Practice of Zen*. New York: Harper and Row, 1959.
2. Kodera, Takashi. *Dogen's Formative Years in China*. Boulder, Colorado: Prajña Press, 1980.
3. Mathews, R. H. *Mathews' Chinese English Dictionary*. Cambridge, Massachusetts: Harvard University Press, 1948.
4. Okumura, Shohaku. *Shikantaza: An Introduction to Zazen*. Kyoto, Japan: Kyoto Soto Zen Center, 1985
5. Sheng-Yen, Master. *The Poetry of Enlightenment: Poems by Ancient Ch'an Masters*. Elmhurst, New York: Dharma Drum Publications, 1987.
6. Soothill, William Edward and Lewis Hodous. *A Dictionary of Chinese Buddhist Terms*. Taipei, Taiwan: Buddhist Cultural Service.
and various and sundry dictionaries, footnotes, hints, etc., in many books.

Physical Postures for Meditation

Rev. Master Daishin Morgan

B y expressing the mind of meditation with your body, you bring both body and mind together in their true unity. The mind needs to be bright and alert so you should sit up straight, but without tension. The spine should have a gentle forward curve in the lumbar region so the torso can be erect, but without strain. To become familiar with the correct position of the torso, stand up straight with your feet together and relax your shoulders and abdomen. Place your forearms in the small of your back and feel how it is possible in this position to relax and yet be standing up straight. There is stability and an immovable quality that has strength without force or hardness. Notice how your hips are rotated forwards in a way that keeps the small of your back curved inwards and allows your abdomen—when it is relaxed—to hang forward.

Meditation on a chair

Next, sit on a chair, preferably a dining chair or piano stool with a flat or nearly flat seat. Arrange a flattish cushion towards the back of the seat and sit down so that the base of your spine is on the cushion. (Make sure the edge of the chair does not press into your thighs.) This, in effect, gives the chair a slight forward tilt which lets the hips rotate forwards as they did when you were standing up straight as described above; your spine will then naturally go into the correctly curved position. Place your forearms in the small of your back again to make sure it feels the same

17

as it did when you were standing straight. Unless you have a back problem that prevents you from sitting straight, do not use the back of the chair for support. Keep your feet and knees apart to give yourself a stable base.

Put your right hand on your lap with your left hand on top (or vice versa if you are left-handed) and put your thumbs together as shown in one of the photographs below. As the meditation period continues, if you become distracted your thumbs will often droop or lose contact with each other as fantasies occupy the mind. If this should happen, you can bring yourself back to the mind of meditation by simply correcting your hand position and posture.

Do not close your eyes as this encourages sleepiness and foggy states of mind; you should keep them open but lowered so that you are looking at a point on the floor or wall roughly three to six feet in front of you. Keep your eyes in focus, but do not pick on one little spot and stare at it. In a sense, you want to keep your eyes in focus but, at the same time, look within. In other words, do not get caught up in what is in front of you; allow your attention to be on the stillness. Blink naturally so that your eyes are under no strain. If you normally wear glasses, keep them on during meditation. Keep your mouth closed with your tongue touching the back of your top teeth; breathe quietly through your nose. Try to breathe naturally using both chest and abdomen so that the breath is deep and quiet, but not exaggerated. The essence of serene reflection meditation is that it is a natural activity that should be done without strain. If you notice you are breathing particularly shallowly, as often happens during periods of anxiety, then deliberately breathe more fully for a minute or two, and then go back to just sitting still. You should not get caught up with physical sensations any more than with thoughts. Although there are physical characteristics of deep meditation, you do not want to try to imitate them—just concentrate on sitting still as outlined and your body will naturally express this stillness in a way that is right for you. Everyone's body is slightly different so please remember that what is described here is a blueprint, not an absolute standard.

Meditation on a bench

Meditation on a cushion

Another position is the kneeling posture with a meditation bench. The bench has a forward-sloping seat that supports the buttocks and prevents the ankles from being crushed or the knees being strained. The legs of the bench should only be long enough to allow the ankles to fit underneath the seat. Too high a bench, or one with too steep an angle, exaggerates the curve of the lower back and causes pain. Some people find that their arms are not long enough to rest comfortably in their lap when using a bench, a problem that is easily solved by placing a small cushion under the hands.

For those who can manage it, the cross-legged postures also provide stable positions for meditation. However, enlightenment does not depend upon sitting cross-legged so do not force yourself into painful positions and end up damaging your knees, hips or back. Approach these positions with care, only using them if they do not cause physical problems and remember that your body is the body of the Buddha and should be respected. All cross-legged positions require a meditation cushion; however, a folded blanket or pillow can be used to experiment with. Whatever you use should provide a firm base to support the tip of your spine about three to five inches off the floor. Only the tip of the spine should rest on the cushion; otherwise the cushion will press into the back of the thighs and cut off circulation.

For the Burmese position place one foot directly in front of you, the bottom of the foot touching the bottom of the opposite thigh and your other foot directly in front of the first. As with all cross-legged positions you will feel very unstable unless you have both knees on the

Meditation in the Burmese position

ground, but it may take a little while for the sinews to stretch sufficiently to allow this to happen. Go carefully and do not force your knees down. This is probably the easiest cross-legged position to get into but it may require some muscular effort to hold the back in the correct position. For those with long legs this position can cause strain on the knees, so use with care.

To sit in the half-lotus position, place one foot in front of you, the bottom of the foot touching the bottom of the opposite thigh and the other foot on the opposite thigh. In the full-lotus position each foot is

Meditation in half lotus

Meditation in full lotus

placed on the opposite thigh. All cross-legged positions cause a slight twist in the spine so it is very important to alternate which leg you have in front to avoid back trouble that otherwise could develop in the future. Most people find it takes a few months before they can sit cross-legged comfortably and without pain for a full meditation period of thirty minuutes. At the outset, gradually ease yourself into the position shown and sit for a short time. If you want to try sitting cross-legged, it is essential to get your posture checked at a meditation group meeting, or at one of our priories or retreats before too long.

When more than one period of seated meditation (which should not be more than forty-five minutes), are scheduled, they are alternated with periods of walking meditation. Each forty-five minute period of seated meditation is followed ideally by a fifteen-minute period of walking meditation: sitting without such movement for longer periods can cause serious physical injury to the feet, knees, hips and back. This is true for all of the postures described above. Walkng meditation also helps us to appreciate that meditation is not dependent on physical immobility: it can be a bridge between formal meditation and meditation within the activities of daily life. It can also be usefully practised if sleepiness becomes a persistent problem.

Get up slowly and gently and commence to do your kin-hin. Kinhin [walking meditation] is done by making a fist of the left hand, with the thumb inside, and covering it with the right hand; it should not be held tightly against the chest wall but in an oval position. The arms, being held loosely, form an oval at the level of the chest with the elbows extended. The body must always be erect with the eyes again still in their naturally lowered position, not closed nor looking too far ahead of the feet....Beginning with the left foot, walk calmly and slowly, with great dignity; do not walk absent-mindedly; a step of not more than six inches at a time should be taken. Walk first on the heel and then along the side of the foot ending upon the toes so that the foot digs itself into the ground as it were. This is done for five to ten minutes after each period of thirty or forty minutes sitting. Remember that this is moving Zazen [meditation]; it is not done [merely] for the purpose of stretching the legs as some people think.[1]

In exactly the same way as when sitting, you just sit, so when walking, just walk. If the mind wanders off, then patiently bring it back to just walking. In this way, mind and body become one and we are able to realise our true nature.

Meditation can also be done whilst lying down, although this position should only be used when illness or disability prevents one from sitting up. The best position is to lie flat on your back with feet together and hands clasped at the chest in the same position as described for walking meditation, except that the hands are allowed to rest against the chest. Some people find it helpful to slowly move

Walking meditation

their feet to help keep awake, and others find it necessary to have their knees slightly raised. Keep your eyes open in a position that corresponds to a downward gaze if you were sitting up.

Once the sitting practice is over, you then get up and attend to whatever needs to be done, doing it with the mind of meditation. If your mind wanders off, you quietly bring it back to the job in hand so that work becomes meditation in exactly the same way as sitting becomes meditation. It is easiest to learn how to make work into meditation with simple, manual activities like walking up and down stairs, washing up, using the lavatory, cleaning the house, etc. Whenever fantasy takes over, recognise what is happening, let go of it, and come back to what you are doing. In time you become a lot more concentrated and this has many beneficial side-effects as you learn to bring the mind of meditation into all activities of life. In the end, meditation truly becomes a twenty-four-hour-a-day activity.

Note

1. Roshi P.T.N.H. Jiyu-Kennett, *Zen is Eternal Life*, 3rd ed. rev. (Mt. Shasta, California: Shasta Abbey Press, 1987), pp. 31–32.

Pure meditation opens us so that
we may directly realize the
Foundation of our minds and dwell content within
our own Buddha Nature.

Great Master Keizan Jokin

The Mind of Meditation

Rev. Master Daishin Morgan

Serene reflection is a method of meditation that can be summarized as 'just sitting'. To just sit still is the simplest of all activities and yet within it we obstruct ourselves with all manner of unnecessary complexities. The essence of serene reflection meditation is to simply *be* without adding anything or taking anything away. It is based on the fundamental teaching of the Mahayana tradition that the Buddha Nature is the foundation of our being. The Buddha Nature is the source of all compassion, love, and wisdom. It is the place from which real love flows out to all without distinguishing one from another. It is this love we all seek, for the ability to give and receive this love is the ability to know perfection, it is the experience of true peace.

The Buddha Nature is not something that exists inside of us like a soul, nor is it something external and apart from us like a god. It is all of existence for it rejects nothing. Infinite compassion, love, and wisdom are the characteristics by which we recognise it but it also embraces what we regard as negative within ourselves and the world around us. The Buddha Nature is enlightenment itself and since it embraces all of existence it includes us. We are not separate from enlightenment but we have mistaken where our true refuge lies. Instead of trusting the Buddha Nature, that which is in tune with all of existence, we take refuge in an illusory sense of self, a self that is fundamentally at war with all of existence. Serene reflection meditation is the means we have of healing the rift we have created between ourselves and the Buddha Nature. Enlightenment is inherent within every one of us, but to know that enlightenment we have to look towards it for our refuge and cease to involve ourselves with greed, hate, and delusion.

Buddha Nature is the essence of stillness; it appears whenever we neither reject nor hang on to anything. To do serene reflection meditation means that you accept everything that arises in stillness,

25

without judgement and without excuse. You must be still with what-ever arises in all its exposed and revealed nature. This is to learn how to see without preconceptions. Meditation is the means we have of coming to know and experience for ourselves that which is true and real. This experience must be direct; that is, it must not take place through filters of past conditioning. If anger arises in meditation we learn to be still with it and simply accept that anger has arisen. We add nothing to it by continuing a series of thoughts about the inci-dent which caused us to get angry, indulging a running commentary justifying our position, going over what we will say next time we meet the person who made us angry, and so on and on. Equally, we do not try to pretend we are not angry by refusing to look at what is actually happening. The way to meditate when anger arises is to sit there and be willing to be angry without judging ourselves as bad or unworthy, and without indulging the anger by carrying on the men-tal jabbering.

To illustrate this I will describe how it feels to come to terms with anger in myself. Having settled myself down to formal seated meditation, a memory from the past comes to mind of a particular incident that made a deep impression on me. There is a lot of anger associated with this memory and, as I find myself getting involved in the apparently inevitable commentary that always seems to ac-company the memory, I become aware that I am involved in a never-ending cycle of thought that just keeps going round and round. I then deliberately let go of the thought process and each time the mind returns to it I simply say to myself quietly and firmly: No, I do not want this, I wish to be still. Since meditation is not a state of vacuity, when I let go of the thoughts I start to become more aware of the underlying feelings. By letting go of the commentary, I start to feel first hand what is actually happening. I become aware of a sense of outrage. To keep the meditation going I must not judge or excuse this, but simply be willing to know the outrage that exists at that moment. This, put another way, means I allow the outrage to be enfolded in the stillness. Complete acceptance is the hall-mark of love; it is there within love that the outrage is embraced. I can now see that the outrage is covering a deep sense of hurt and grief. To continue meditating, I must allow the grief to arise and be still within it, allowing this, too, to be embraced within the loving acceptance that is the stillness. I then become aware, not in words but by simply seeing it unfolding, that behind the hurt and grief lies a fear that I am inadequate and in some fundamental way will never measure up. Again this knowledge is not to be falsely anaesthetised by justification, or by rushing off to prove it is not true by desperately seeking some external worth in the eyes of others. Instead, just as before, this deep sense of inadequacy must be embraced; I must sit there and feel inadequate without running away. When I do this something quite remarkable then takes place. I realise that there is something beneath the inadequacy, I begin to see there is something infinitely still and accepting that embraces all of this—I cannot say it is me, I cannot say it is not me—it is just that when I am still all that arises is embraced within a great loving acceptance. I am embraced within it, it is all of me and there is nothing inadequate, there never has been, and there never will be.

This is what it means to just sit still. When this is done the anger I started with has led me directly to the Eternal Buddha, the Buddha Nature. Thus I begin to understand how it is that there is nothing outside the Eternal Buddha, even that which at first sight seems negative. Indeed, all things point to the Truth when they are looked at with the eye of meditation.

There is not necessarily a strong and powerful memory that comes to mind every time you sit down for formal meditation. Many people experience longish periods where nothing very much seems to happen. Some people even sit for years and years waiting for something to happen and it never seems to. This is a condition in which one needs to learn to look deeper at what is going on. There is always plenty happening within meditation but we have to learn how to see it.

I mentioned earlier the importance of having the body in an alert position. This is because mind and body are not separate things; if the body is alert it helps to keep the mind bright. In a similar kind of way all the layers of delusion we get involved in give rise to corresponding tensions within the body. Very often these tensions, or some of them at least, become apparent in the abdomen area. When you take up your sitting position you need to relax your abdomen, let your stomach hang out. When we try to achieve this relaxed posture we become aware of tensions in this area. We are unable to just relax; there is a bit of a knot in there we do not seem able to let go of. For many people it can seem as though there is a whole web of tensions preventing the abdomen from returning to its naturally relaxed position. If you start to get all worried about these tensions you only add to them. They come about because we constantly try to present an image to ourselves and to the world that is not accurate. We feel our self-respect depends upon the maintenance of this image and so we are very afraid of letting it go. The way forward is to just be aware that the tensions exist, and, as it were, cradle them within the loving acceptance I spoke of earlier. If you have your hands in the recommended position for formal meditation they are at the level of or below the navel; your arms surround the abdomen and all its tensions and it is as though your arms are the all-embracing arms of the Buddha Nature. Just be still within this loving acceptance and do not try to make the tensions go away or you will end up playing the same old game. Just be still and embrace the tension, being willing for it to be there. When you do this you find that the tensions begin to unlock; you begin to see directly what causes them without a lot of discursive thought. I must stress that this is not analysis but looking directly, embracing. You will begin to see what the causes are but you may not be able to put them into words. That does not matter in the least—what matters is that you unlock the tensions.

Just as happened with the anger, so in this case the tension itself reveals to us what lies beneath it. When we touch, or rather when we are touched by the Eternal, then we know that a refuge exists that is beyond any image. It is a true refuge that nothing can destroy. The beauty of it is that we find the refuge by means of what, at first sight, is the very obstacle that keeps us from it! Whatever arises within meditation, be it the sense of great compassion or boiling hate, by simply being still and not indulging it, we are lead by it directly to the Eternal. There are no real obstacles provided we keep meditating. There is no substitute for practice where meditation is concerned; you come to understand what it is and how it works by doing it, and by doing it regularly.

The result of doing meditation is that you become aware of many things in your life that need to be changed. If you wish to go deeper with your practice, then those changes will need to be made. There is no limit to how far the practice goes and in the end we have to give up everything. I do not mean we must rush out and give away all we possess—it is actually much harder than that. You have, in the end, to come to a place where you go beyond all you have known in the past. Some people experience this in meditation as approaching a cliff edge which you know you need to step over, but you cannot see if there is anything there to hold you. Most of us turn tail at this point and hide. It is important then not to condemn ourselves, but accept the fear within the same loving acceptance. We then find ourselves returning to that cliff edge and maybe we turn and run again, but in time we approach it, and, almost before we realise what has happened, we step off; we let go of all that we believe ourselves to be and trust the Eternal absolutely. We then find we are within the hand of the Eternal Buddha and always were. What we have had to give up is the clinging to the idea that we are separate. Once we know we are in the hand of the Eternal, there is an end to fear. If life comes, there is life; if death comes, there is death: we are free to live fully and freely without the tyranny of fear. I have yet to meet someone who was able to take this leap without having a few 'trial runs' at the first. We all have within us what it takes to train, we lack for nothing, but it takes time to grow the necessary faith in ourselves and the Eternal. All we need for the great work is at hand; meditation is the means we have of discovering it.

Some people worry that meditation is a way of hiding from the world, but, on the contrary, through coming to understand one's true relationship with the Eternal Buddha and all beings, you begin to see more clearly where your resposibilities lie. Meditation is not an antisocial activity, quite the reverse; it is the still point of certainty, the source of strength that enables one to act with compassion and wisdom, which are unfettered by fear. However, one's practice should not become obsessive; a sense of humour should be maintained whilst still understanding the great seriousness of the work. Most people have so many commitments that there is little chance of their practice becoming obsessive, but in these days of unemployment some may find themselves with a great deal of time on their hands. Meditation is a very valuable use of this time, but remember that meditation is for oneself and for all beings as well. One needs to give in practical forms expression to the compassion that arises in meditation. It is not a good idea to spend hours and hours doing one's own practice in isolation from the rest of the world. This can lead one to lose perspective on reality. Remember to maintain a balance between formal meditation and practical meditation (meditation in action). Even monks living in a monastery do not spend their whole day doing formal meditation, and much time is spent in practical activities that benefit others.

The Heart of Meditation

Rev. Master Meian Elbert

[This is an edited transcript of a talk given on July 26, 2012, during a lay retreat at Shasta Abbey that focused on meditation practice. It was first published in the Journal of the Order of Buddhist Contemplatives, Spring 2013 with the title "Serene Reflection Meditation."]

Today I'm going to talk a bit about meditation practice. We all know basically how to sit, and we all know more or less what we're supposed to be doing, and we all know that it's hard to do. Our form of meditation— Serene Reflection, shikantaza, just sitting— is difficult to describe. It's very simple, and yet it's subtle and it's not easy to grasp. When it comes down to it, we just allow ourselves to fall into it in a certain way—it's hard to do it too deliberately—and it's different for everybody: everybody meditates slightly differently. We all sit a little differently; we experience it quite differently. People who teach meditation each teach it a little differently. It's not a hard and fast thing; it's fluid and dynamic.

For some people meditation is simple: sit down, look at a wall—fine, they seem to get it right away. For others of us— maybe for most of us— it's hard. We can spend years trying to figure out what we're supposed to be doing, or why we're constantly distracted, or what we're supposed to be doing with our mind: "And if I really want to meditate, why is it so hard and why do I keep getting distracted, or falling asleep, or why do I have pain ?" It's just not an easy thing for many of us.

To practice Serene Reflection Meditation is really jumping in the deep end, because it's formless. Most meditation practices have more structure: You count your breaths, or you have a mantra, or a koan, or you visualize a Buddha or a Bodhisattva. Or you contemplate the parts of the body or you reflect on death. There are all kinds of things that many traditions do in their meditation practice. Strictly speaking we don't do any of these things: we just sit.

However, sometimes it is useful to use some extra method to help us to anchor the mind. Because of the formlessness of our meditation it's hard to grasp, so sometimes it's helpful for some of us to count the breaths if we're really distracted or we're just beginning. Or maybe to do it occasionally when the mind's all over the place, or regularly at the beginning of meditation. If it helps, it's fine. Eventually, it's nice if you can let go of counting breaths and just sit. For some of us, following the breath without counting works well. There are various other ways we can help to focus the mind, but fundamentally we just sit. Serene Reflection Meditation is "the Dharma Gate of repose and joy," as Dogen calls it. Actually, we're lucky, because although it's hard and subtle, it's a wonderful practice; and in fact many other forms of practice eventually come down to doing what we actually try to do from the start —to just sit.

So how do we 'just sit?' Where do we put our energy and our focus? I have found that the best thing for me is to sit wholeheartedly in the body: just sit in the body. There's a phrase that Rev. Master Daishin Morgan uses in one of his books, "Fully occupy your body."[1] I find this very helpful. Put your energy into just sitting there in the body, the whole of the body, not focusing on any part of the body. It's a vital, dynamic practice. We're not just sitting there passively, as if we were watching TV. We're sitting there with energy and a certain kind of effort. It takes a while to get this—for it to mesh as it were. It's not forcing, we're not trying to get something or achieve something. We put our energy into just sitting fully in the body. To do this, we need to commit ourselves completely to just sitting, here, in this body, in this very moment. We have nothing to do; we have nowhere to go. All we have is this very moment, right now. And we need to invest in it fully, because this is our very life. At this moment right now, all we have is this moment, right here, in this body, in this breath.

Uchiyama Roshi wrote a lovely book called *Opening the Hand of Thought*,[2] which has some good instructions on meditation, and he says, "Doing zazen [or meditation] means taking the correct posture and entrusting everything to it." Entrusting everything to it: this doesn't mean we have to have some perfect posture. We can sit on a cushion, on a bench, on a chair, we can lie down, we can stand, we can walk. All of these things are pure meditation, if we commit ourselves to it fully, entrusting ourselves to it. It's this wholehearted commitment that is the point. We keep coming back to being here in this body: "Am I sitting up straight? Are my eyes open? Am I relaxed or am I knotted up in some way?" If there are things we habitually slide into — leaning over to one side or hunching our shoulders or closing our eyes — we just need to check now and then to make sure that we're upright, relaxed, alert, without constantly worrying about our posture. We can just be aware of what we're doing, that we are sitting up straight, awake, alert; and yet not tense, not forcing, not trying to get something. We put our whole vitality into it, and then relax ever so slightly so we're not striving against something; we're not trying to push our way through some door. We're just sitting, wholeheartedly, in this very body, in this very breath.

We put our energy into sitting in the body, and don't worry too much about what the mind is up to. This is why I think sitting in the body is so helpful, because we can get all wound up in our mind, 'thinking about thinking about thinking.' When we notice we're distracted, we just come back. We don't have to get all worried about what we're thinking about, or worried that we're thinking, or worried that we shouldn't be thinking. Just come back, just relinquish the grip and come back (this is easier said than done).

Sometimes we're in turmoil about something. We're upset about what someone's done, or what we've just done, or we're confused and afraid, or we just have a lot of emotion coming up. This is all fine, we don't have to fix it. We don't have to try to calm the mind. Don't try to calm the mind because it's like trying to smooth out pancake batter with your hand — you just get it all sticky and everywhere and it makes it much worse. Just leave it be and let it settle of itself, even if it doesn't seem to settle down right away. Not pushing things away, or squashing them down, but just not stirring them up. Just let them come up and go through. As I said, easier said than done, because sometimes turmoil just seems to go on and on. We're really upset about something and we chew it over and over and over, and we can't seem to let it go. Just be patient. Just let it come up, and try not to feed it with the mind. If we're angry it doesn't help to keep going over and over and over the event, think-ing about what we're going to say to the person next time we see them, or justifying ourselves in some way. That just feeds it and makes it worse. Let the anger be there, without feeding it. Let it be there in the body, just feel it in the body. Accept it with kindness. It's not a problem that it has arisen. It's what we do with it that counts, neither holding on nor pushing away; neither gripping on and feeding it, nor trying to squash it down or get rid of it, thinking it's bad.

We sit in the body, with whatever is there, with patience and not with judgment; with kindness to ourselves and to others—pa-tience, kindness, compassion. Not thinking, "I shouldn't be like this. I should be calm. I'm supposed to be meditating." We just let it all come and go—with kindness and acceptance—as best we can. It's not always easy; we just do our best and trust that that will work, that it is sufficient.

A lot of the time we simply have thoughts arise, not particu-larly emotional thoughts, but just thoughts, distracting thoughts, and we tend to follow them. "Oh, I should have done this. Oh, I need to do that. Oh, this other thing that happened the other day." We're pulled off by the endless drooling mind. When we notice we've gotten distracted, we just come back. When our intention is just to sit, when this is the most important thing we are doing at this moment, our distraction vanishes in an instant. It just disappears, because it has no reality. It's just a thought; it's not a real thing. It's just our thinking mind. When we notice: "Oh!" — just come back. When we're invested in our thinking it's harder to let it go — "I real-ly need to remember to do such and such," or, "I really must sort out this problem" — then it sticks to us. But if we can just trust that the most important thing, right now, is to sit here no matter what, and that we can attend to all these other things later, then we can come right back, and we aren't pulled off so much. This is partly a matter of will, and yet it's not just will. It can be quite hard to relinquish something that we've just thought of and feel is really important. Then we ask, "What is really important?"— just sit, right here, right now, and let everything else fall into place after that. We commit ourselves to simply sitting, here in this body, not grasping after our thoughts — opening the hand of thought, as Uchiyama Roshi calls it — relinquishing the grip. It's gripping onto the thoughts that's the problem; then we follow them and get pulled off. But if we just open that hand, and see that they are not the most important thing, then they just slide right through and we're not pulled around by them.

I think the most important section in Great Master Dogen's "Rules for Meditation" is, "Sit steadily, neither trying to think nor trying not to think; just sitting, with no deliberate thought, is the important aspect of serene reflection meditation."[3] This is just what we have been talking about: sitting steadily, "neither trying to think nor trying not to think." That's how Rev. Master Jiyu put it in her translation, and it's a really helpful way to look at it. You're not investing in your thoughts and you're not trying to push them away. Sitting steadily in the body—wholeheartedly; just sitting, fully present, in this moment, with this breath, right now.

We're not trying to attain some perfectly controlled state where we have no distracting thoughts. We tend to think we should be in some perfect samadhi where we're just peaceful and blissful. But we're not trying to get to some perfect place. Our meditation is dynamic; we sit still and yet it's constantly moving and flowing. As I sometimes have said, it's like sailing a boat: we're constantly moving, constantly adjusting to the wind, to the slight movement of the body and the mind. It's something that we're continually doing, coming back to the body, sitting still, sitting upright, entrusting ourselves to the posture, to the practice, to our own commitment, to our effort. Someone I know who's been meditating for many years, not in our Order but in a similar Soto Zen tradition said, "It seems I'm always going away and coming back." He is not locked into some perfect static place. This person is deeply devoted to meditation, has been doing it for many many years, sits for long hours, and sits like a rock — impressive — and yet he's always going away and always coming back. Always distracting thoughts can arise and always the person brings themself back. It's dynamic, constantly moving, you're never there: "Here I am, I've arrived." We're always "going on, going on, always becoming Buddha"[4], always continuing our training: it's never perfect. We can't say: "I'm satis-fied. This is fine, now I know what I'm doing and I can just lock down in this position and here we are." We're always having to make that effort, the adjustment to the wind.

Don't get discouraged if meditation seems really hard. I know all about meditation seeming really hard: It still works. Don't worry about the thoughts: "My meditation is terrible…" or, "I'm no good at this." Don't worry about it, it still works, this is the wonderful thing about it. Despite our best effort, despite our view, despite the ideals we may have, despite our expectations, it still works. It changes us in a profound and subtle way. We don't know how it works, it just does. We just have to get out of the way and let the meditation do its work. We set up the conditions, we try our best to do our part: something else does the rest. There is something that helps us. Sometimes it seems like we fall easily into meditation and sometimes we're just struggling to stay awake, or we're just con-stantly distracted, and we can get discouraged. But do not worry, because it still works, it still helps us. There is something that helps us that is more than just our little struggling self trying to do its best. There is something bigger that helps.

We need to let go of all expectation—of ourselves, of our med-itation practice, all ideals, all standards. We're not trying to get something. We're not trying to get anything. We're not trying to have experiences or get enlightenment. If we have experiences of insight, or blissful states, or anything else, it's fine. They can be very helpful, as long as we don't grab at them and try to hold onto them, or try to get them back. It never works, you never get back to it, because you're always moving forward. It's like trying to get back to that point on the sea you just left—it's gone. Just keep mov-ing forward: we can't get back to the moment before. To try to get back or to grab onto some ideal is missing the point. All we can do is set up the conditions: do our part, try to do our best, and trust it. Have faith in the practice: the meditation does us, it's not us doing the meditation. It's bigger than us; it works in spite of us.

Our way is the gradual way. It's not a quick fix—there isn't a quick fix. Meditation can make a huge difference in our lives, and quite quickly. But its effects are subtle and profound, and they can take years to ripen. It's not the dramatic experiences and insights that help us most. They can take years to understand and make use of and incorporate into our lives. That's done through our daily practice: our daily meditation, our daily training in sitting still, keeping to the Precepts—all the things we do. Many of us don't have dramatic experiences at all. We just keep on doing the training faithfully, and that is what counts; training without expecting something—just giving ourselves to it.

We're not trying to get something; we're giving ourselves to something—completely. The more we give ourselves to our practice, the more it rewards us; but we don't do it to get rewards. The other day I was talking to somebody about their job and how rewarding it is to work just for the sake of doing the job well, and not for the sake of rewards—of getting a lot of money for it. Meditation and training are like this. We do it for its own sake, not to get something out of it. And there is joy in it. Yet we don't do it because of expectations or ideals, we do it because it is good to do. We do it because it is our true heart's desire: all of us know this. We train because we have to train, because it's what we need to do. It's the purpose of our life, fundamentally. We follow that true heart's desire, go where it leads us, without expectation, without ideals, without seeking some perfect static place. We keep on faithfully walking the way, because it is good to do, because it is our true heart's desire.

Serene Reflection Meditation, "the Dharma Gate of repose and joy." May it be so for all of us, as we give ourselves to it.

Notes

1. Morgan, Rev. Master Daishin Morgan, *Sitting Buddha: Zen Meditation for Everyone*, (Throssel Hole Press, UK, 2004).
2. Uchiyama, Kosho, *Opening the Hand of Thought: Foundations of Zen Buddhist Practice*, (Somerville, MA: Wisdom Publications, 2004).
3. Dogen, "Rules for Meditation", on p. 1 of this book.
4. *The Scripture of Great Wisdom, The Liturgy of the Order of Budhist Comtemplatives for the Laity*, (Mt. Shasta, CA: Shasta Abbey Press, 1990), pp. 97–100.

Possible Physical Problems
Met with in Meditation

Peter Lavin

When we sit we take refuge in the Three Treasures. It is easy to see that we are taking refuge in our own Buddha nature (not that this is separate from everyone else's) but we should also remember that we take refuge in the Dharma and in the Sangha. We should be aware, too, that we need to find the middle way, the path between the opposites.

As far as the physical side of meditation is concerned, the Sangha can help us make sure that we have as correct a posture as our body allows. At the outset we should ask a priest to check the way we are sitting. If, later, problems arise we should make sure that these are not caused by our sitting improperly, and it is always good to check with a priest when any apparent difficulty arises.

We take refuge in the Dharma during meditation by listening to all the teaching that comes to us, and this includes through our body. As we begin to sit up straight in the presence of the Buddhas and Ancestors our body often complains that we are pushing it into un-accustomed shapes. Here we need to find the line between giving in too easily to discomfort and causing ourselves unnecessary pain. As a general rule we should sit still with the ache until we really have to move and then change to a comfortable position with as little fuss as possible. If, however, we find the pain persists we should seek advice from a priest or, if appropriate, a doctor.

There is no need to sit cross-legged, which usually results in aching knees and ankles if we are not used to it, but, if we do, it is essential that we alternate the position of our legs each time we sit to avoid permanent damage to the spine or hips. Generally our body will warn us if we are causing it lasting harm but this is not always the case. It is good to examine in detail why we are sitting cross-legged if that is what we choose to do.

38

Discomfort may also come from being too tense. This can often result in pains in the back or shoulders. Here again we need to find the balance between holding ourselves stiffly erect and sagging. Once we have straightened our backs we should relax our body but make sure our mind is still alert. The tenseness or laxity of our thumbs in the meditation mudra during meditation is a good indication of whether we are too tense or too relaxed.

If we find that our legs have gone to sleep during the meditation period, we have probably been cutting off the circulation by sitting too far back on our seat or pressing one leg on top of the other. A small cushion on the chair can raise the bottom sufficiently to prevent this. Legs that have fallen asleep buckle under the weight of standing, so to prevent winding up on the floor, always make sure that the circulation to the legs is normal *before* trying to stand. Sometimes they can fall asleep without our being aware of it.

In the beginning we may be distracted by certain physical effects. It can take a little practice to keep the eyes focussed on the wall in front of us without getting caught by patterns or shadows, or going off into a slightly trance-like unfocussed state. At times the wall may appear closer or further away than we know it is. As soon as we are aware of any of these we simply need to bring our mind back to just sitting, perhaps blink once or twice, and focus our eyes on the wall without examining it in detail. If we usually wear glasses to focus our eyes at that distance we should wear them for meditation and our eyes should be allowed to blink in the usual way; otherwise we may find they begin to water.

Drowsiness is something that can arise because we are tired or for reasons that are not so easy to understand. Sitting in a well-ventilated room that is not too hot and trying to find time for our meditation before the end of the day can help here. If we find that we are falling asleep for no apparent reason we probably need to experiment to find what works for us. Some people find that putting their hands in gassho until the drowsiness passes helps. For others a repeated act of will may be called for (perhaps asking the help of Achalanatha,[1] for we are never sitting alone). We may need to remind ourselves of why we have come to our sitting place and make sure our mind is bright and positive.

Meditation can only be learnt by doing it and it is a continuing process. Just as we sit and let the thoughts come and go, so can we let the physical distractions come and go: if we are sitting properly, our Buddha nature will draw our attention to those we should pay heed to, and that is when to take refuge in the Three Treasures.

Note

1. Achalanatha, the Unmoving Lord (J: Fudo-myo-o), is one of the Guardians of the Gateways to training. He represents one aspect of the Eternal—the will to train, to sit still and be unmoved by anything within or outside of ourselves. We can call on the help of this aspect of the Eternal and find that place within each of us that is immovable, imperturbable, indestructible.

Your Place of Meditation

Rev. Master Shiko Rom

The means of training are thousandfold, but pure meditation must be done.[1]

A lthough meditation can be done everywhere, it is very helpful to have a place set aside in your home for doing formal meditation. In monasteries, the meditation and ceremony halls are decorated carefully and beautifully to help strengthen faith in what they represent—the beauty inherent in all existence, the Unborn (Buddha Nature) which is found within ourselves and all things. They are kept neat and clean and treated with great respect. In setting up your own sitting place, you can keep these attitudes in mind; for in doing so, you are encouraged to believe that there is something beautiful within yourself and all things, something that is worthy of care and respect.

Setting up an altar and meditation room

Keep in mind that you want to make the place in which you do formal meditation the least distracting and most conducive to meditation as possible. The ideal is to have a quiet room in your home that is used only for meditation. If this is not possible, a part of a room that will not be used for anything else during your meditation periods—a corner of your bedroom or living room, for example—will work fine. It is not always possible to find a place that is completely quiet: you may hear traffic, a dog barking occasionally, people walking by. You can learn to meditate with a certain amount of noise; however, you want to avoid being around such things as television, music or loud talking, which can be very distracting especially to someone new to meditation.

A small altar, as a reminder of the Unborn and one's purpose for training, is often placed in the meditation room or near one's sitting place. The altar itself can be a small table, a wall-mounted

41

shelf or a specially-made altar cabinet. A statue or picture of a Buddha or some aspect of the Unborn, such as Great Compassion (Avalokiteshwara Bodhisattva), Great Love (Samantahadra Bodhisattva) or Great Wisdom (Manjusri Bodhisattva) is placed in the center at the back. To symbolize the blossoming of enlightenment, flowers are placed to the left of the statue and, out of concern for all living things, artificial flowers or potted plants are used

Guest office altar at Shasta Abbey

instead of cut ones. A candle or altar light is placed on the right side, signifying the light of Eternal Wisdom. Placed directly in front of the statue or picture, a water-offering cup expresses the cleansing aspect of the Unborn. An incense burner is in front of the water-offering cup, the offering of incense representing gratitude for the Three Treasures: the Buddha (the historical Buddha, Shakyamuni, and one's own Buddha Nature), the Dharma (the teaching transmitted through Shakyamuni Buddha), and the Sangha (those who live by the Buddha's teaching). Vegetarian offerings, such as fresh or dried fruit, nuts, prepared food, or artificial food, may be placed on the altar as well, representing the willingness to share the benefits of training with all beings.

If you are meditating on the floor and your room is not carpeted, it is advisable to place a large flat cushion or piece of carpeting beneath your meditation cushion or bench to help prevent pains in the legs and knees. You want to have the temperature in the room within a comfortable range, preferably on the cool side. One or two windows for natural light and air circulation are good. The lighting should be gentle: during the day, light from a window will probably be sufficient; when it is dark, a candle, small lamp or altar light can be used. Meditation is an inward-looking process; for that reason we meditate facing a wall, and it should be as non-distracting as possible.

Clothing

Body and mind are one. Your outward appearance reflects your inward state of mind and can help or hinder your meditation. If you sit up straight, are clean and dressed neatly, you not only convey a bright, positive attitude, but you are also more likely to find that brightness and positivity. The clothing worn for meditation should be clean, respectful and comfortable. Loose-fitting clothing is advisable—slacks that do not put pressure around the waist or restrict circulation when the legs are bent or a long skirt that is full enough to allow the legs to be bent underneath. Do not wear bed-clothing (except when meditating as you go to sleep or when ill).

The meditation period

Treat your sitting place with respect. At the monastery, we bow as we enter or leave the meditation hall, thus showing gratitude for having a nice place to sit. We then bow to our sitting place (cushion, bench, or chair) and turn around and bow to everyone else who is meditating with us. Once seated, we bow again to begin and end the meditation period. This helps us in many ways: when we bow we express our gratitude, and the act of bowing itself helps us to find that gratitude; it helps us bring ourselves together when we feel scattered; and it helps us bow to our Greater Selves, for it is only when we put our trust in that which is greater than ourselves, the Unborn, that we find what we are looking for. Even when sitting alone, we can still bow "to others" before and after sitting, thus recognizing that we train for both ourselves and others and that we are grateful for the training of others.

Before each meditation period you can offer incense at the altar (or simply in an incense burner if you do not have an altar),

blessing the incense by touching the base of the incense stick to
your forehead and reciting the Three Homages aloud or to yourself
("Homage to the Buddha; Homage to the Dharma; Homage to the
Sangha") before putting it into the incense burner.[2] You may time
the meditation period by the burning of the incense stick or you
can time it with an hour-glass or a gentle-sounding alarm clock or
watch. If a few people are meditating together, usually one person
times the meditation period, ringing a gong to begin and end it. After
you stand up from meditation, you again bow to your seat and bow
outwards to everyone else. You may also wish to recite a Scripture
and offertory verse before or after a meditation period, Great Master
Dogen's "Rules for Meditation" being a very useful one.

When to meditate

At Shasta Abbey we sit formally when we first get up in the
morning and currently at 7:15 pm in the evening. Rising time varies during the year: during formal monastic terms, it is usually at 5
am. Some people find that on first arising in the morning their minds
tend to be bright and positive. The Buddha Nature within us is always bright and positive; through old habits, likes, dislikes, opinions and the like, we create clouds that cover up this brightness. I
have found that when I am freshly awakened from sleep in the early
morning, the clouds are fewer or have not yet formed, and I am able
to see the brightness and feel faith more easily. Meditation in the
evening can help us see and let go of whatever has been happening
during the day and renew our faith if events have obscured it. These
times may not be possible for you: find what fits into your schedule
so that you will actually be able to meditate on a regular basis; you
can do seated, formal meditation any time during the day except for
the forty-five minutes or so after a meal when your food is digesting.
When you first start, you may only want to sit for five or ten
minutes and gradually work up to twenty or thirty minutes once or
twice a day. It is better to start out slowly than to overdo it at first
and then lose interest; but, try to meditate every day, if only for a
few minutes, as it is important to commit yourself to a regular practice—the times when you least feel like meditating can be the times

of greatest benefit. You can meditate formally once or twice a day, or more often, if you have the time, although you should not meditate for longer than forty-five minutes without a period of walking meditation and possibly a short rest. You can also take a few minutes periodically throughout the day wherever you are to bring yourself back to the stillness of meditation and get in touch again with what really matters. No matter how busy your life may seem, you can always find the time and place to meditate if you really want to.[3]

The purpose of having a special place for meditation that you care for and respect is so that you can begin to open the door to your True Self and learn to show respect for all things. However, the Eternal can be found everywhere and in all circumstances, and we eventually discover that the true meditation hall is within our own hearts and that we carry it with us wherever we go. The priest Nyogen Senzaki wrote:

> Like a snail I carry
> My humble Zendo[4] with me.
> It is not as small as it looks,
> For the boundless sky joins it
> When I open a window.[5]

Notes

1. *Rules for Meditation.*
2. At Shasta Abbey, we no longer burn incense indoors except during a few of our ceremonies, because a number of people have trouble with the fumes. We offer unlit incense in the Hall and then burn it in a safe place outside afterwards.
3. It is inadvisable to spend many hours in formal meditation to the neglect of one's responsibilities or spend hour upon hour in formal meditation on one's own, without the direction of a qualified spiritual teacher.
4. Meditation Hall.
5. Quoted from *Like a Dream, Like a Fantasy: The Zen Writings and Translations of Nyogen Senzaki*, edited and with an introduction by Eido Shimano Roshi and published in 1978.

Children and Meditation

Rev. Master Jiyu-Kennett

I am often asked, "How do you teach meditation to children and what is the best age to start at?" In the east the average child is taught to meditate as soon as it is possible for it to sit upright; i.e. around one or two years old. No doctrine is put into the child's head. The mother and father, and the rest of the family, will sit quietly in front of the family altar; the child, without being restrained, will either sit for a few moments or roll around on the floor with the parents taking no notice. The parents thus express their knowledge of the child's latent understanding and do not treat it as less than themselves. In a very short time the child wants to sit like the parents, as do, interestingly enough, the dog and cat. I have sat down to meditate and my cat has come up, looked at the wall and then sat down to look at it with me. Thus, if the parents meditate, the child will meditate too. I have seen children at the age of two and a half doing formal meditation in the laymen's meditation hall in Sojiji—and doing a wonderful job. I have photographs of them. These children do a meditation so pure and exquisite it is unbelievable to watch; but they would not be able to discuss the Buddha Nature with you, nor would they be able to put into words the doctrine of the Trikaya— nor would they be able to explain the "all is one" and the "all is different" that their little bodies express. Their explanations are not as the world understands explanations. And yet every part of their bodies will express the "all is one" and the "all is different"—they will express the Buddha Nature for they have learned to meditate with their whole being untrammelled by duality. They are indeed whole creatures and can teach us much.

From "The Education of the Buddhist Child" by Rev. Roshi Jiyu-Kennett; reprinted from *The Journal of Shasta Abbey*, December 1974: 12–16.

Every-minute Meditation

Rev. Master Daizui MacPhillamy

Most students of Buddhism know that the practice of meditation is not something which is limited to the times each day we spend in formal seated meditation. But to bring the mind of meditation out of the meditation hall and into our everyday world of work and daily living is not always an easy thing to do. I would like to share with you a method for helping to do this. It is a practice common to many schools of Buddhism and is known variously as "mindfulness training", "working meditation", or "every-minute meditation". The method can be summarized in five steps:

1. Do one thing at a time.
2. Pay attention to what you are doing.
3. When your mind wanders to something else, bring it back.
4. Repeat step number three a few hundred thousand times.
5. But, if your mind keeps wandering to the same thing over and over, stop for a minute; maybe it is trying to tell you something important.

That is all there is to it. It is incredibly simple and requires nothing more than the willingness to do it with some persistence, yet, at least for me, it has been second only to formal seated meditation as the most important method of practice in my training.

The reason for step number one is not hard to see: if we accept that Truth is One and undivided, then It can only be realized by a mind which is itself unified and aware. Such one-pointedness and mindfulness are, by definition, impossible when you are doing two things at once or are not paying attention to what you are doing. Thus, if you choose to try this practice, it means no more eating

Reprinted, with changes, from *The Journal of Shasta Abbey*, vol. XII, nos. 5 and 6: 18–22.

breakfast, talking to your spouse, and watching "Good Morning America" all at the same time; planning your ten o'clock meeting while you drive to work is out; so are thinking about skiing while you do the dishes, reading a magazine while you're on the toilet, and worrying about your finances while you plant your garden.

This practice, you will note, is exactly what the schedule, rules, and ceremonial of a training monastery help one to do. For the new trainee in a monastery, the opportunities to learn this art are considerable. He or she does so naturally if he simply follows the schedule and keeps his mind on what he is doing. The postulancy and novitiate are times in a monastic career when the method of every-minute meditation can be most easily practiced. Not all of us, however, are attracted to a monastic vocation, and even those who are so inclined do not remain beginning trainees forever. For most people, therefore, the task is a little harder because there are usually many things which we could (or, worse yet, should) be doing at any given time, and the temptation to do more than one of them is great. A person in this position may find it helpful to add a "step zero" before the first step. Step zero is to decide what is the one most important thing to be doing at this particular moment; then, do it.

Not only must we do one thing at a time, but also we must pay attention to the one thing that we are doing. This attention should be the same as that used in formal seated meditation. One must not exclude thoughts, perceptions, emotions, etc.; yet whenever one is aware of having become attached to, or enmeshed in, them, one brings one's mind back to focus on the task at hand. It is very important to understand this statement. Mindfulness training is not the same as focusing the concentration upon one object to the exclusion of all other things. That would be simply a different way to create a duality, to divide up the world. It would also be dangerous: people who exclude things from their awareness tend to deceive themselves and to have accidents. This, by the way, is one means the teachers in a Buddhist monastery have of knowing if the students are doing the practice of mindfulness correctly. If they are doing it right, they become more efficient at their jobs; if they've got it backwards, they start having accidents or become inefficient. So, you exclude nothing from awareness, but when you realize that you have become distracted, then your attention is gently returned to the present activity. This is repeated hundreds, perhaps thousands, of times a day, and there is a certain amount of trial and error involved in learning how to do it correctly.

So much for steps number one through four. They are not hard to understand; with them it is really mostly a matter of whether or not one decides to do them. Step five, however, requires more exploration. Occasionally a thought just will not leave you alone. No matter how many times you bring your mind back to the business at hand, this thought keeps insisting itself upon your consciousness. There is sometimes a good reason for this: the thought is trying to tell you something. What I do in this circumstance is to stop what I am doing and take that "bothersome" thought seriously for a moment. In other words, I make thinking about that topic the one thing I am doing: I switch my attention to it and cease doing what I was doing before. The most common causes for such persistent thoughts are that there is something else that you could be doing which is more urgent than what you were working on at the time, that there is something left unfinished or wrong or dangerous in what you are doing, or that there is a nice ripe insight waiting to come into your awareness. If none of these things seem to be the case and there does not appear to be anything further to be learned from examining the thought, then switch your attention back to what you were doing before. If the thought still keeps coming up, allow yourself to stop again after a while and look at it another time, and so forth.

This ability to switch one's attention from one activity to another readily and without attachment does not come easily for most of us. With practice, it can be cultivated. In a training monastery the schedule is designed to help one learn this: when the bell sounds one stops what one is doing, bows, and goes to the next thing. You might think of certain aspects of your life as this bell: "intruding" but important thoughts, the boss's request to change everything you've just done, or the baby's crying. They are signals to "bow" and switch your attention to something else. I sometimes liken mindfulness training to driving on an icy road: keep a gentle, smooth control of the wheel, keep your eyes on the road—but don't ignore your peripheral vision, and when you see a truck skidding towards you, change course gently and don't insist on the right-of-way!

There are two common objections to the practice of every-minute meditation. The first is, "I'll never get my work done if I do only one thing at a time." This is a reasonable concern; fortunately it is usually unfounded. What actually happens for most people (after the initial few days of awkwardness when the whole thing can seem a bit strange and disruptive of one's habitual patterns of living) is that they can actually do more and better work by doing one thing at a time. I think what happens is that the time saved when one does several things at once is more than compensated for by the increased efficiency (and decreased tension) that results from devoting all of one's attention to the task at hand.

The second objection is that doing this is a lot of work and it interferes with customary social interactions. This is true, and it is for these reasons that I do not recommend doing it all the time, at least not for most people. Even in the monastic setting, a certain rest from this practice is built into the system, and the monks enjoy social conversation while drinking tea or eating an informal meal in the refectory. So, perhaps you may choose to eat breakfast and talk to your spouse at the same time, after all. Go ahead, and enjoy the meal together (but I'll bet you enjoy it more if you don't also try watching TV at the same time).

My advice, therefore, is to do one thing at a time (and pay attention to it) as much as it seems wise to do so, bring your mind back gently each time it wanders, but don't be so strict on yourself that you find the practice unpalatable. Done properly, the exercise of every-minute meditation is refreshing, liberating, and energizing. Together with formal seated meditation, it can make a significant contribution to increasing one's religious understanding. It is my favorite form of meditation.

The Buddhist Precepts

Rev. Master Daizui MacPhillamy

[This is part of an article written by Rev. Master Daizui in 2001 on the Noble Eightfold Path. The full article can be found on the OBC website: obcon.org –ed.]

The Four Noble Truths

The first of these is that life as we normally live it doesn't really make us very happy or peaceful in the long run. First of all, we're never satisfied: if we don't have something, we want it; if we have some, we want more; and if we have lots, we're both afraid of losing it and we also see that there is something even more that we could get, which we then want. This is true not only of material things but also of relationships, reputation, … most everything. This pull of greed and push of fear leave little room for lasting contentment. Secondly, we actually do lose things, and that hurts: we get sick, we have misfortunes, we are separated from those we love, we die.

The second Noble Truth is that there is a cause for the frustration and suffering: the fact that we hold on to things, grasp after them, are attached to them. What actually hurts is not that we don't have something; it is that we don't have it and we want it. What causes grief is not that we lose something; it is that we are unable to accept the fact and let go.

These observations lead directly to the fact that there is something we can do about all this. We can't stop the way the world works (although much of what we do seems to be an attempt at just this), but we can change how we relate to it. If we could just find a way to give up our grabbing on to things, find a way to accept life as it actually is, then peace, contentment, and real happiness would naturally be there. This is the third of the Noble Truths, and the fact that there is a way of actually doing this is the fourth. That Way is the Eightfold Path itself. These Four Noble Truths are the core and essence of Buddhism, the very observations which led Shakyamuni Buddha all the way to enlightenment....

The Precepts

The three aspects of the Eightfold Path which are concerned with speech, action, and livelihood form a group, known as Sila. They form a guide to how to live one's life so as to make every action accord with enlightenment. When we practice sila, we train from our outward actions towards inward peace, just as when we practice meditation and mindfulness we train from our inward acts of mind toward outward harmony with the universe. These two approaches complement each other and lead towards a unified Buddhist life. Over the centuries, Zen has taken the various elements originally assigned to the ancient path factors of speech, action, and livelihood, and has developed and reorganized them into sets of precepts. There are a number of ways of expressing these precepts; what follows is but one. While at first glance precepts can appear to be rigid rules of conventional morality, in fact they are guides to liberation. Taken as descriptions of enlightened behavior rather than simply as proscriptions against evil acts, they lead to the signs of wisdom — charity, tenderness, benevolence, and empathy — rather than to guilt, shame, or self-blame. Those who make a life of right speech, action, and livelihood find that they become more aware of their own spiritual heart; those who ignore them find that a coarsening and closing off occurs, both in their spiritual life and in relationships to other people.

The Three Treasures Precept

The Three Refuges, shared by all Buddhists, are the first and most general precept of all.

"I take refuge in the Buddha." I entrust my life to the guidance of both the Buddhas who have appeared in this world and the Buddha Nature within.

"I take refuge in the Dharma." I go for direction to the teachings of all those who have walked this Way before me.

"I take refuge in the Sangha." I seek the advice and wise counsel of those who share the love of truth and commitment to the Eightfold Path.

When taken together as one ongoing precept, as one unified way of life, the Three Refuges will guide and harmonize our understanding of all of the other precepts. If any one of them is left out, our training is like a stool with only two legs: unstable and sure to fall flat.

The Three Pure Precepts

These offer a means of interpretation for the specific precepts to follow and guidance in situations where no specific precept seems to apply, or where precepts seem to conflict.

"I will cease from evil." First and foremost, it is my wish to harm no living thing. I will ask in the innermost place of my heart, "Is what I am about to do a harmful thing, a thing which places any separation between a being and the Unborn? Is it a thing which is to be abstained from, a wrongful thing, an unwise thing?" In one sense, "evil" does not exist: there are only unwise actions, done in ignorance and confusion. I pray that I may not do any such thing, whether to myself, others, or the world.

"I will do only good." It is my sincere wish to do only that which accords with the truth. I will ask in the innermost place of my heart, "Is what I am about to do fitting, suitable, a thing to be done? Does it tend towards liberation?" This is the good that goes beyond the opposites of "good" and "evil".

"I will do good for others." I pray that my every act will be of true benefit and that I may never inadvertently create conditions which may lead others to do harm. I will ask in the innermost place of my heart, "Is what I am about to do truly of use? Is it a fit offering? Does it accord with the purification of my heart?"

If we can honestly say that in any matter of importance we have considered carefully these Three Pure Precepts, then we can rest in the knowledge that we have done our best. And that is all which Buddhism ever asks of us. Mistakes will still be made, of course, for we are human. But they will have been made with a pure heart, and in the big perspective, that matters. There are many ways to consult the quiet, still, innermost place of the heart. Each of us must do this honestly, as best we can. There are no formulas, no easy answers. Never trivialize the Three Pure Precepts.

The Ten Great Precepts

These ten are specific guidelines for the Buddhist life, as undertaken by the Zen trainee. When they become our blood and bones, we are a true child of Buddha. When we deliberately ignore any of them, we create a separation between ourselves and the family of Buddha.

"I will refrain from killing." Since all beings are one within the Buddha Mind, how could I willingly cut off the life of any creature?

"I will refrain from stealing." Since it is my true wish to give up all attachments, how could I willingly grasp after anything which is not freely given?

"I will refrain from abusing sexuality." Since physical affection is a deep expression of love, and love is an aspect of the Unborn, how could I willingly debase this sacred love by merely gratifying my desires in a way which uses, harms, betrays, or abuses anyone?

"I will refrain from speaking untruthfully." Since my heart's desire is to be one with truth, how could I willingly deceive anyone by any means whatsoever?

"I will refrain from selling the wine of delusion. Since clear awareness is the door to enlightenment, how could I willingly hinder the Way for anyone by enticing them into partaking of substances, ideologies, false beliefs, or anything whatsoever which befuddles or intoxicates?

"I will refrain from speaking against others." Since it is my wish to live by the compassion within my heart, how could I willingly speak hurtfully or disparagingly about anyone?

"I will refrain from being proud of myself and belittling others." Since the false notion of self is the very thing I seek to abandon, how could I willingly inflate it with pride, much less do so through seeking to denigrate others?

"I will refrain from holding back in giving either Dharma or wealth." Since charity is the first sign of enlightened action, how could I practice stinginess in any form whatsoever?

"I will refrain from indulging anger." Since it is my heart's wish to let the love within it flow forth unboundedly, how could I hold on to and nourish angers and resentments which may arise, much less act openly upon them to cause harm?

"I will refrain from defaming the Three Treasures." Since these are my true refuge and the very Way, how could I turn from them myself, much less cause doubt about them to arise in others?

Kyojukaimon and Commentary
Giving and Receiving the Teaching
of the Precepts

Great Master Eihei Dogen
Commentary* by Rev. Master Jiyu-Kennett

Preceptor:–

"The Great Precepts of the Buddhas are kept carefully by the Buddhas; Buddhas give them to Buddhas, Ancestors give them to Ancestors. The Transmission of the Precepts is beyond the three existences of past, present and future; enlightenment ranges from time eternal and <u>is</u> even now. Shakyamuni Buddha, our Lord, Transmitted the Precepts to Makakashyo and he Transmitted them to Ananda; thus the Precepts have been Transmitted to me in the eighty-fourth generation. I am now going to give them to you, in order to show my gratitude for the compassion of the Buddhas, and thus make them the eyes of all sentient beings; this is the meaning of the Transmission of the Living Wisdom of the Buddhas. I am going to pray for the Buddha's guidance and you should make confession and be given the Precepts. Please recite this verse after me:–

Preceptor followed by congregation:–

"All wrong actions, behaviour and karma, perpetrated by me from time immemorial, have been, and are, caused by greed, anger and delusion which have no beginning, born of my body, mouth and will; I now make full and open confession thereof.

*The words of Great Master Dogen's *Kyojukaimon* have been enclosed in double quotation marks to distinguish them from Rev. Master Jiyu-Kennett's commentary. For this reason, within the commentary itself, single quotation marks have been used for material that normally would have been enclosed in double quotation marks.

Preceptor alone:–

"Now, by the guidance of the Buddhas and Ancestors, we
can discard and purify all our karma of body, mouth and
will and obtain great immaculacy; this is by the power of
confession.

"You should now be converted to Buddha, Dharma and
Sangha. In the Three Treasures there are three merits; the first is the
true source of the Three Treasures;"—there is an Unborn, Uncre-
ated, Unformed, Undying, Indestructible, the Lord of the House,
That which speaks in silence and in stillness, the 'still, small voice.'
"The second merit is the presence in the past of Shakyamuni
Buddha"—all Those Who have truly transmitted Buddhism through-
out eternity.
"The third is His presence at the present time,"—all Those
Who transmit the Truth, Who live by the Precepts and make them
Their blood and bones, the Sangha, the embodiment of the Precep-
tual Truth of the Buddhas.
"The highest Truth is called the Buddha Treasure,"—the knowl-
edge of That Which Is, the knowledge of the Unformed, Uncreated,
Unborn, Undying, Indestructible; the certainty, without doubt, of
Its existence, the knowledge of It within oneself, the Buddha liv-
ing within oneself, the Lord of the House Who directs all things. If
you study true Buddhism you will become as the water wherein the
Dragon dwells; it is necessary to know the true Dragon; it is necessary to ask the Dragon, the Lord of the House, at all times to help
and to teach. Only if you give all that is required of the price that the
Dragon asks will He show you the jewel; you must accept the jewel
from the Dragon without doubting its value or querying the price.
"Immaculacy is called the Dharma Treasure,"—one must live
with the roots of karma cut away. To do this we must indeed know
the housebuilder of this house of ego, know all his tools, know all
his building materials; there is no other way that we can know immaculacy. The housebuilder of the house of ego must be known absolutely, recognised at all times. It is not enough to have a kensho;
one must go back to the source of the karmic stream; one must return to that source to find out what set it going. Kensho shows the

slate is clean; to find the source of karma cuts its roots and, with constant training, keeps evil karma at a minimum but, since there is nothing from the first, there is nothing clean and nothing that is unclean—we cannot know this, however, until we have first tried to clean it. 'Most houses can do with a thorough sweeping but even a million sweepings will not clear away the dust completely.' Thus man remains in his body and accepts it, knowing that <u>nothing matters</u>, that he is immaculate, always was and always will be. This is the immaculacy of the Dharma Treasure; this makes the immaculacy and harmony of the Sangha Treasure possible. It is the knowledge of the True Kesa, that which is immaculate above all dust and dirt, the knowledge that the dust and dirt are indeed a figment of one's own ego's imagination as a result of past, accrued karma, that makes possible the Transmission of the Light from the far past to the now and the far future without words. The Scriptures show up blank pages; there <u>is</u> a Transmission that lies beyond them.

"Harmony is the Sangha Treasure"—this is brought about by the knowledge that, no matter what a member of the Sangha may do, he <u>is</u> immaculate from the very beginning; there <u>is</u> nothing from the first. 'Thus shall ye think of all this fleeting world, a star at dawn, a bubble in a stream, a child's laugh, a phantasm, a dream.' Although this is true the members of the Sangha, the Zen Masters, all beings are bound by the law of karma; they will pay the price of what they do. Thus is the mind of the Sangha Treasure.

"The person who has realised the Truth really is called the Buddha Treasure;"—he <u>is</u> the embodiment of the Truth, he <u>is</u> Nirvana, he <u>is</u> the Embodiment of Enlightenment, he <u>is</u> the Treasure of the Buddha for, in him, can be seen fully-digested, Preceptual Truth.

"The Truth that is realised by Buddha is called the Dharma Treasure,"—that is the <u>knowledge</u> of the Unborn, Uncreated, Unformed, Undying, Indestructible; the living with this knowledge without doubt, the trusting eternally of the Lord of the House, the certainty of the Treasure House within oneself at the gate of which sits the True Dragon Who <u>is</u> indeed the Lord of the House.

"The people who study that which lies within the Treasure House are called the Treasure of the Sangha,"—the Dharma and the Sangha are one and the same thing, being the embodiment each of the other, if fully-digested, Preceptual Truth is their rule of life. If you ask, 'What is a monk?' you <u>know</u> that it is his Kesa.

"He who teaches devas and humans is called the Buddha Treasure,"—he who gives true teaching, being beyond praise and blame, the holy and the unholy, right and wrong, without fear or favor, he who becomes 'good' for others.

"That which appears in the world in the Scriptures and is 'good' for others is called the Dharma Treasure,"—anything may teach. However infinitesimally small, however large, no matter what, all things may teach the Dharma when they live by fully-digested, Preceptual Truth, when they have cut away the roots of karma, when they know the housebuilder of the house of ego and are constantly keeping him from rebuilding again as a result of <u>practising</u> fully-digested Preceptual Truth.

"He who is released from all suffering and is beyond the world is called the Sangha Treasure;"—he for whom no longer desires burn, wherein wants and cravings no longer exist; he who gets up in the morning and goes to sleep at night, eats when he is hungry, sleeps when he is tired, is satisfied with that which he is given and does not ask for more than he can absolutely use in the immediate now. When someone is converted to the Three Treasures thus, he can have the Precepts of the Buddhas absolutely.

In this manner you should make the True Buddha your teacher and not follow wrong ways. The True Buddha that is your Teacher is indeed the Lord of the House, the True Dragon. Do not hold on to your tiny kensho; trust the Lord of the House, hold fast by Him no matter what state you may be in, whether you are well or sick, brightly alive or dying, hold fast by the Lord of the House.

The Three Pure Precepts

"Cease from evil.

> This is the house of all the laws of Buddha; this is the source of all the laws of Buddha." The law of karma is one of the five laws of the universe; it is absolute, it is inescapable. All are bound by the law of karma once it is

set in motion. By accident someone made the course of
karma; it is not intentionally set in motion; what happens,
or happened, or will happen to you or to anyone else is
caused by karma; by accident the wheel rolled the wrong
way. Do not continue the rolling of the wheel in the wrong
direction by dwelling on the past or fearing the future; live
now without evil. Stop the wheel <u>now</u> by cutting the roots
of karma, by knowing the housebuilder of the house of
ego; if you do not, karma will go on endlessly. The only
difference between you and another being is that <u>you</u> have
the opportunity of knowing the Lord of the House right
now, having heard the teachings of the Buddha. Others
may have less opportunity than you but, when they hear
it, who knows which will be first at the gate of the Treasure House? 'Cease from evil' is absolute, in thought, in
word, in deed, in body, in spirit. All are bound by the law
of karma; do not doubt this. You will pay for everything
you do if you do not cut the roots <u>now</u> and live by fully-
digested, Preceptual Truth. Do not worry about the karma
of others; each man his karma makes.

"Do only good.

The Dharma of Shakyamuni Buddha's Enlightenment is
the Dharma of all existence." Do not do anything unless it
is 'good;' do not do anything unless you have first asked
the Lord of the House if it is good for you to do it. Do
nothing whatsoever in a hurry; do nothing whatsoever on
the spur of the moment unless you know the <u>certainty</u> giv-
en by the Lord of the House; know that you must take the
consequences of what you do if it is not a fully-digested
act for <u>you</u> know What lies beyond good and evil, right
and wrong; <u>you</u> know That which lies beyond morality;
you <u>know</u> the Lord of the House. Ask the Lord of the
House at all times before you do anything whatsoever. 'Is
it good? Is it Your will?' If you do not ask the Lord of the
House, the housebuilder of the house of ego will again

pick up his tools and, before you know it, there will be
a great structure from which you must again escape. If
a thing is 'good' in this way it may be done; if it is not
'good' in this way it should not be done; I am not speaking here of good and evil; I am speaking of 'good' in the
sense of if it is right; this is beyond right and wrong; if it
is good is beyond good and evil. This teaching is indeed
the teaching of Shakyamuni Buddha's enlightenment for
there was not one of His acts that was not the result of
fully-digested, Preceptual Truth. If you live thus, doing
that only which is 'good' after you have asked the Lord
of the House, after you know the true Lord of the House,
then you can know the teaching of Shakyamuni Buddha's
enlightenment and know that His enlightenment and
yours are identically the same; but this is only if you know
who the Lord of the House is and do not suffer from the
idea that you are the Lord of the House. Always you must
ask the Lord of the House; always you must be humble in
His presence. 'Please teach me that which it is good for
me to do this day. Please show me that which it is good
for me to teach this day. Please give me the certainty that
I teach the Truth and know, indeed, that when the still,
small voice within my mind and heart says "Yes," I must
obey that teaching. When it says "No," I must not disobey
that teaching.' When the Lord speaks, spring up joyfully
to answer; then, indeed, it is good to do anything whatsoever He asks; know that the Lord will never break the
Precepts.[1]

"Do good for others.

Be beyond both the holy and the unholy. Let us rescue ourselves and others." Do not set up a chain of causation that
will cause others to do wrong; do not do that which will
cause another to grieve; do not do that which will result
in your creating karma for another being; do not accidentally set the wheel of karma in motion. Do not let yourself

hear the words, 'What demon allowed you to become a priest? From what demon did you learn Buddhism?' To be beyond both the holy and the unholy, to be beyond praise and blame, to act only from what the Lord of the House teaches without worrying whatsoever what the world may think is indeed to have understood the Three Pure Precepts. Before any act is performed you must ask yourself, 'Am I ceasing from evil in doing this act? Is it good in the sight of the Lord of the House? Shall I cause another being to do harm either to himself or to others? I cannot stop <u>him</u> doing harm, for each man his karma makes and must carry for himself, but I can do that about myself which will prevent <u>me</u> from accidentally starting the course of karma. I must think carefully of my every act. I may not cause another to make a mistake in Buddhism.' By so doing we rescue both ourselves and others for, in cutting the roots of karma for ourselves, we help to cut the roots of karma for others also.

"These three are called the Three Pure Precepts." Without them one cannot live the Buddhist life.

The Ten Great Precepts

"Do not kill.

No life can be cut off for the Life of Buddha is increasing. Continue the Life of Buddha and do not kill Buddha." Above all, do not turn your face away from Buddha, the Lord of the House, for this is indeed to commit spiritual suicide; to kill Buddha is to turn away from Buddha. 'Man stands in his own shadow and wonders why it is dark and only he can turn round.' To turn away from Buddha is to say, 'My ego is greater than the Lord of the House; my opinions are more right; my wishes are more important.' It is <u>you</u> whom you kill. If you do not listen to the Lord of the House in this life, in what life will you listen to the Lord of the House? Will you for eternity attempt to commit <u>real</u> suicide? If you always face the Buddha you will always know Buddha; if you always listen to the Lord of the House there is no possibility of your ever killing anything.

"Do not steal.

> The mind and its object are one. The gateway to en-lightenment stands open wide." There is nothing whatso-ever that can be stolen. 'Preserve well for you now have,' says the Scripture; each of us possesses the Treasure House. All we have to do is ask the Dragon for permis-sion to enter, ask the Dragon if we may see the jewel and it will be given to us. He who tries to rob himself, he who tries to steal from the Treasure House can never have the Treasure; erudition is as this; taking drugs is as this. All you have to do is ask the Lord of the House and you may know and possess all things. The gateway to enlighten-ment does indeed stand open wide for the true mind of the Buddha and the jewel are one and the same; ask the Lord of the House at all times. Remember that 'he who counts another's treasure can never have his own;' he who steals can only ever rob himself.

"Do not covet.

> The doer, the doing and that which has the doing done to it are immaculate therefore there is no desire. It is the same doing as that of the Buddhas." Thus there is nothing to be coveted and no one that covets. 'Preserve well for you now <u>have</u>,' says the Scripture. Since there is nothing from the first, how can there be anything to preserve well? 'The white snow falls upon the silver plate; the snowy heron in the bright moon hides; resembles each the other yet these two are not the same.' Thus we think there is a difference; thus we think there is an ability to covet and something <u>to</u> covet; thus man makes mistakes. Indeed there <u>is</u> nothing from the first.

"Do not say that which is not true.

> The Wheel of the Dharma rolls constantly and lacks for nothing yet needs something." The Dharma is Truth itself but it needs expression. He who lies does not allow the Dharma to show itself, he does not allow the Dharma to be expressed, he does not allow the world to <u>see</u> the Dharma Wheel in action. And still the sweet dew covers the whole world, including those who lie, and within that dew lies the Truth.

"Do not sell the wine of delusion.

> There is nothing to be deluded about. If we realise this we are enlightenment itself." 'Thus shall ye think of all this fleeting world, a star at dawn, a bubble in a stream, a child's laugh, a phantasm, a dream.' If you hold on to nothing whatsoever there can be no delusion nor can there be enlightenment; then there are no opposites. Thus, indeed, we are enlightenment itself—yet always we will have the form and figure of old monks.

"Do not speak against others."

> Do not speak against the Lord of the House. Every person, every being <u>is</u> the Temple of the Lord wherein the Lord dwells, the still water wherein the Dragon lives. If you speak against others you speak against the Lord of the House. Do not try to divide the Lord of the House; do not try to cause war within the Lord; do not try to make the Lord make war upon Himself. "In Buddhism, the Truth and everything are the same; the same law, the same enlightenment and the same behaviour. Do not allow any one to speak of another's faults." Do not find fault with the Lord of the House. "Do not allow any one to make a mistake in Buddhism." To speak against the Lord of the House is the gravest mistake of which I know.

"Do not be proud of yourself and devalue others."

It is enough for me to <u>know</u> the Lord of the House, to know that He dwells within all things. How can there be devaluation of others if they are the Temple of the Lord? How can there be pride if all possess equally within the Lord? "Every Buddha and every Ancestor realises that he is the same as the limitless sky and as great as the universe. When they realise their true body there is nothing within or without; when they realise their true body they are nowhere more upon the earth." There is nothing to be proud of and nothing to be devalued.

"Do not be mean in giving either Dharma or wealth."

Since all possess the Lord, there is nothing to be given and nothing to be taken away, and still all things must be given, all things offered at all times and in all places. "One phrase, one verse, the hundred grasses,"—all contain the Lord, all express the Lord—each in its own way and each perfectly. "One Dharma, one enlightenment, every Buddha, every Ancestor." No difference, nothing greater, nothing smaller; nothing truer, nothing less true. When all is within the Lord, all stand straight together, a million Buddhas stand in one straight line. Out of gratitude to the Buddhas and Ancestors we give Dharma, we give wealth, we give life itself—strength, youth, beauty, wealth, everything that we have and, even then, we cannot give thanks enough for one second of their true training; we can never repay their kindness to us. Only by our own true training is this possible and then, again, there is no repayment; it is just the work of a Buddha.

"Do not be angry.

There is no retiring, no going, no Truth, no lie; there is a brilliant sea of clouds, there is a dignified sea of clouds." Just there is that going on which causes us to see unclearly;

but if we truly look, if we look with care, we will see that the true and beautiful sky is shining behind the clouds; we may see the Lord of the House. No matter how angry the person is who is with us, we may see in him, too, the Lord if we are truly looking, if our own ego is out of the way and, in seeing the Lord in him, he can see the Lord in us. The depth of the ocean is still even when there is a great storm upon its surface; thus should we be when there is anger, knowing that nothing whatsoever can touch the Truth.

"Do not defame the Three Treasures.

To do something by ourselves, without copying others, is to become an example to the world and the merit of doing such a thing becomes the source of all wisdom. Do not criticise but accept everything." The Lord of the House does not always do things in the normally accepted ways, nor do the Buddhas and Ancestors; they are not individual and they are not the same as each other. Each expresses the Truth in his own way as do all things; they do that which they do in their way and express the Lord within it. Do not criticise the way of another, do not call it into question; look within it and see the Lord. Look with the mind of a Buddha and you will see the heart of a Buddha. To criticise is to defame the Lord of the House. Love the Lord of the House at all times—know Him, talk to Him; never let a day go by when you do not consult with Him even on the slightest matter. Then you will never, as long as you live, defame the Three Treasures.

"These sixteen Precepts are thus.
Be obedient to the teaching and its giving; accept it with bows."

Note

1. When one 'asks the Lord', one should know that the Lord will <u>never</u> tell you to break the Precepts—any of them; if you hear to the contrary, the voice you are hearing is the voice of self and not the voice of the Lord. The teaching given in this paragraph must not be taken out of context and either made into a quick and easy substitute for full Preceptual inquiry or applied to trivial things. There are brief periods in training when a Preceptual review of <u>every</u> action is advisable in order to deepen one's understanding of the Precepts; at such times the teaching of this chapter is applied to every act one does. At all other times it is important that one be <u>willing</u> to apply it to all things and at the same time be both practical and spiritually mature in reserving this type of inquiry for truly important matters, while accepting the responsibility for using the Ten Precepts and one's wise discernment to guide one's behaviour in everyday matters.

Whenever one does 'ask the Lord', one must <u>also</u> do <u>all</u> of the other aspects mentioned in this chapter, including carefully considering the likely consequences of one's proposed actions, comparing those actions to the Ten Precepts and other Scriptures and, especially, consulting and following the advice of the Sangha. To do only part of this is to fail to take Refuge in the Three Treasures; such a course of action is contrary to Buddhist teaching. Be warned: there are no shortcuts to Buddhist training and all people, including full Zen Masters, will reap the karma of their actions. [JK]

Reading the "Kyojukaimon and Commentary"

David Powers, Lay Minister

O ne of the most useful and powerful parts of my training is the daily reading of the *Kyojukaimon and Commentary*, the sixteen Precepts, together with the commentary of Great Master Dogen and of Rev. Master Jiyu-Kennett. When I first began reading the *Kyojukaimon and Commentary*, I must say I had only a very foggy idea of what it was about. But as I continued to read it and meditate, things began to become more clear. Sometimes one of the Precepts has seemed to come to life and stand out in relief as I went about my daily business. The two particular Precepts with which this has happened are:

"Do not speak against others."

Do not speak against the Lord of the House. Every person, every being is the Temple of the Lord wherein the Lord dwells, the still water wherein the Dragon lives. If you speak against others you speak against the Lord of the House. Do not try to divide the Lord of the House; do not try to cause war within the Lord; do not try to make the Lord make war upon Himself. "In Buddhism, the Truth and everything are the same; the same law, the same enlightenment and the same behaviour. Do not allow any one to speak of another's faults." Do not find fault with the Lord of the House. "Do not allow any one to make a mistake in Buddhism." To speak against the Lord of the House is the gravest mistake of which I know.

This article first appeared in the *Berkeley Buddhist Priory Newsletter*, Fall, 1981.

"Do not be proud of yourself and devalue others."

It is enough for me to <u>know</u> the Lord of the House, to know that He dwells within all things. How can there be devaluation of others if they are the Temple of the Lord? How can there be pride if all possess equally within the Lord? "Every Buddha and every Ancestor realises that He is the same as the limitless sky and as great as the universe. When They realise Their true body there is nothing within or without; when They realise Their true body They are nowhere more upon the earth." There is nothing to be proud of and nothing to be devalued.[1]

One day I began to realize that I was breaking these Precepts time after time during the day, so I started to make an effort to keep them. The first thing that happened was that I found I had about twenty-five to fifty percent less to say during my normal conversations when I quit judging, criticizing or making fun of others. Although dramatic, this change was not too difficult, once I made the effort. However, the next level in keeping the first of these Precepts was much more subtle and difficult. I would find myself listening to others criticize someone else and to some extent supporting them just by nodding my head slightly or rolling my eyes or with a facial expression that indicated consent. These little gestures of consent would frequently result in two or three minutes of breaking the Precepts with criticism. When I began to stop doing this the effect it had on my interactions was surprising, and after a while people tended not to run someone or something down when I was around.

Reading the *Kyojukaimon and Commentary* has also had other effects. For example, there have been times when I was just about to do something (or in the middle of it) when one of the Precepts would come to mind, like, "Cease from evil." At these times the Precepts have kept me out of a fair amount of trouble. At other times I have been pondering over a decision (like, should I write off this lunch as a business expense or was it social?), when I just stop and turn to the Precepts. There is "Do not steal," and the decision is suddenly easier. I do not have to think, "Will I be audited by the IRS, and if so can I prove that we talked about business?" The truth is it was just a friendly lunch, not business, and the decision is that simple.

It is important when putting the Precepts into practice to use them as a guide to avoid mistakes and not to use them to be unnecessarily harsh with oneself. For example, in the above case it is useful to recognize that declaring a lunch as a business expense, when it is not, would be making a mistake. However there is no benefit in going beyond this and saying that I am training poorly because I almost broke the Precepts and therefore I am *bad*. It can be a very severe mistake to misuse the Precepts in this way, and in fact one is actually breaking the Precepts by so doing. I have found the Precepts to be most helpful when used as a gentle guide to point the way when faced with the decisions and problems of everyday life. It is not possible to keep all of the Precepts literally at all times, but we must do the very best we can.

One of the things that surprised me about trying to keep the Precepts was that some of them actually get a little easier with practice. A good example is anger. When I started out trying not to get angry it seemed almost impossible. This was because when I realized that I was angry, the anger was already overwhelming. It was like trying to stop Niagara Falls. But with some persistence, I began to notice my anger as it started to arise. When I was able to see the anger arising, it also became easier not to get caught up in it. The anger did not disappear, but I did not necessarily have to do anything with it, such as yell at someone or defend myself. Sometimes the anger just comes and goes very quickly when I recognize it and do not get tangled up in it and feed energy into it. This is like a large boulder sitting at the top of a hill. Once the boulder starts to roll down the hill it gathers momentum and becomes more and more difficult to stop. But if you watch the boulder very carefully at the top of the hill and see when it just begins to teeter, you can steady it without too much effort. Trying to keep the Precepts is like carefully watching the boulder. The more you practice, the better you get at keeping the boulder balanced and seeing when it starts to teeter. In this way one of the big problems that comes up for me is now much easier to train with than it was when I first started.

The thing that is most helpful to me about reading and taking the Precepts is that I can do it now. I do not have to wait until I have more faith, or until I decide if I want to be a monk, or until I go to a meditation retreat or until everything is *just right*. The Precepts are something that I can put into my everyday training now and they get straight to the heart of what I am trying to do. Reading the *Kyojukaimon and Commentary* takes me about twenty to thirty minutes. It is important to read in a place where there is as little distraction as possible and to give yourself fully to reading without the diversion of a cup of coffee or conversation. Reading just before meditation, or just after, also seems to be helpful. I try to read the *Kyojukaimon and Commentary* every day, or half one day and half the next if there is not time all at once. I am sure that it would also be helpful to read it twice a week or once a week if that is all the time one can find. The benefit seems to come from reading and practicing on a regular basis so that the Precepts weave themselves into the fabric of our everyday life in the same way that daily meditation does.

Note

1. See Great Master Dogen and Rev. Master Jiyu-Kennett, *Kyojukaimon and Commentary*, in this publication.

Continuing Practice after a Retreat

Paul Taylor, Lay Minister

[This article is based on a talk given on the last day of an introductory retreat weekend at Throssel Hole Buddhist Abbey in 2011. It was first published in the Journal of the Order of Buddhist Contemplatives, Winter 2011–12.]

This is intended mainly for those who are quite new to practice though I hope some aspects may be helpful in a wider sense. Each of us continues to train with the sorts of issues discussed here, no matter how many retreats we have attended.

If we decide we want to live from a meditative perspective when we return home from a retreat, how do we go about doing this? It can feel strange going from the all-round supportive atmosphere of the monastery or temple to the normal pulls and resistances of our ordinary daily life. It is normal to have contradictory feelings on leaving a retreat, particularly when we are not used to retreats. We might feel a strong sense of relief, of being let off the leash after days of disciplined living. We might feel a bit of a 'come down' and a bit low. Such feelings are not surprising given the intensity with which we have thrown ourselves into the retreat. I usually feel deeply encouraged after a retreat, but I also feel physically pretty tired, and this tiredness can last a while.

It can be challenging re-entering our normal life. Most of us need a bit of time to 'come to' and to re-establish contact. We may be going from a silent reflective atmosphere to a noisier one. Those we return to may be apprehensive of how we may be after a retreat. We may feel like reading the paper, eating cake, watching TV, not unpacking our bag, all at once! 'Phew, I don't have to do it'. Or we may feel a strong urge to tell everyone what we experienced. We may feel a bit grumpy, or we may need to accept others feeling a bit grumpy that we've been away. So what do we do? We can pause: what's good to do here? It may really help to show some appreciation and to make contact with those we return to. Perhaps we can find a low key way to relax without swamping ourselves. We need to let things settle. Re-entering needs care and kindness, for everyone's sake. There may well be time to tell people what we've been doing, but better as it arises naturally, or when they ask.

Grounding in the fundamentals

Having taken part in such a variety of events at the monastery or temple, it may feel confusing as to how we should integrate these into our daily life. So much has happened. I've found it helpful to keep things simple, and to ground myself in the fundamentals. So, my focus has been on setting up and continuing a regular meditation practice, on doing my best to keep in harmony with the Precepts, and on being as kind to myself as I can when I fall over. I need to find a steady pace in my practice I can walk at, and not hold myself on too tight a rein.

When we do this, other things can always be brought in to enrich the fundamentals as and when they help. I have found it helpful to trust that, if I ground myself in the fundamentals, what is useful from my experience at the monastery or temple will naturally be absorbed and integrated into my daily practice. I don't try to remember it or to reproduce the forms.

Regular sitting

Most importantly we need to cultivate a regular meditation practice without being too idealistic. Some regular meditation each day helps: a length of time we can sustain in our lives as they are, morning and evening if we can. A splurge once or twice a week is not quite so helpful. It is also important not to compare and to judge (adversely) how much we are able to sit with what we did on the retreat, and to be content with doing our best. We do need to be sensitive to how it might look to people we live with, if we were to suddenly rearrange the furniture, insist on quietness, and leap out of bed early every morning. It may be better some mornings not to get up early and to spend time relaxing together, and maybe to sit later.

Those around us may not understand too much about meditation. Thankfully, the listening, receptive quality of meditative awareness itself is always accessible to us, moment by moment, as we gradually learn how to integrate meditation into our daily life. Whilst it is certainly very helpful to find or set up a quiet and encouraging space to meditate, we need to be really careful not to communicate to others through our actions that we are trying to get away from or are irritated with them.

Personally I don't eat silent meals normally, but I can always find ways of being more attentive at meals as they are, maybe in listening to others when they are talking to me. My meditation varies in timing and length and sometimes, because of circumstances, I don't get to sit for as long as usual. There is no need to be rigid — intention and willingness are the key.

Allowing our perspective to change

Over time our meditating regularly subtly changes the way we look at things, opening a deeper and more inclusive perspective. However enthusiastic we may be, we can't will our way into this. If we persevere it creeps up on us. We don't need to fear losing it. I used to be afraid, on leaving a retreat, that my daily life was so chaotic and messy, that both I and it were not good enough to make progress. We need to be kind and patient with ourselves if we notice such a sense of desperation, and not act on it. We can take heart: nothing can make us train, and, nothing can stop us training. We find the heart of practice just where we are. The circumstances of our lives, now, are the appropriate vehicle for deepening our practice.

Respecting others

We choose to work on ourselves. It is a mistake to insist that others train. Whilst enthusiasm helps, people tend to back off from 'evangelical' meditators, 'evangelical' non-smokers, 'evangelical' vegetarians, whatever. We all tend to back off when we are lectured at on what we ought to do and what is wrong with us! As we continue to meditate we can just let things emerge and not rush to judgement. We can 'feel out' what response is most helpful and compassionate in each situation. Great Master Dogen tells us that the signs of Enlightenment are generosity, tenderness, benevolence and sympathy. As we go on, we may even find that aspects we thought of as the most difficult and most unpromising in our lives, can turn out to be the most helpful. Meditation enables us to thaw and untangle.

Training with the Precepts

In doing my best to live by the Precepts I have found training with their spirit is important. I break the Precepts where I wilfully, carelessly, or gratuitously, put myself in situations where I know I have difficulties with pulls and resistances. However, I don't break the Precepts when I find myself in seemingly very similar situations where such situations have arisen from how my life genuinely emerges. Then such seemingly unpromising situations become teaching. I don't need to climb mountains if I have a fear of heights. But if I am with friends on holiday and we are walking together up a hill it may be good to join them. Occasionally I need to stand firm. And still, I can find ways to be true to my heart in ways that are sensitive to others: how we do things is often just as important as what we do. As we go on, a changed perspective creeps up on us and we, too, change. If I don't persevere and am lazy, I will continue to gouge out my habitual grooves, in unawareness and suffering. But, if I do persevere, even when I fall over I really don't need to beat myself up. Rather I just need to come back to being present again and again, listening, and then go from here. It is never too late to pause, to listen, and to follow the inner compass of meditation in daily life.

Meditating in activity

I've always really appreciated Soto Zen's emphasis on integrating meditation practice with an ordinary daily life: each reflects the other, and meditating in activity is no less important than sitting meditation[1]. Through our practising meditating in activity we refine our capacity for being receptive and responsive: being receptive to what comes, with openness, flexibility and good grace; and responding wholeheartedly in as collected a way as we can manage. We offer our willingness and our best effort. When meditating in activity[2] we often focus on a particular task. And, because meditative awareness is inclusive awareness, we find ourselves, at the same time, naturally aware in a background way of what is happening inside us and out-side us — a gentle 'listening'. We can trust this awareness and don't need to strive to be aware. It seems to be all going along well. Then we notice our mind has wandered and we have got 'caught up'. We just simply 'come back', again being responsive to the present situ-ation and its needs. This is true whether it is a particular task or a more complex situation which may call us to respond to a variety of different needs in a short space of time. Such more complex situ-ations really test our willingness to let go of each aspect at the ap-propriate moment, and to continue 'listening' for what is needed. We learn more quickly when we have compassion for our mistakes. What we 'come back' to can be varied — it could include planning and assessing our priorities, or honouring a nagging sense that we need to offer quiet space for a while to what is going on inside us.

In this process we may catch glimpses of long-time habits of mind, resistances, attractions, pulls, anxieties; one example may be how we compare ourselves with others. I sometimes notice a ten-dency to become goal-obsessed. Whilst getting an overview of the task in hand can be helpful, I find it doesn't help me to 'glue' my eyes too much on the goal at the expense of tripping over my feet. We may notice a tendency to want to squeeze just that last bit in, to push, to finish off, past what is good, at the expense of the next activity. It is important to be honest with ourselves and at the same time, kind, when we notice we are doing this.

I find that certain working bases for trust really help to point me to the bigger picture in meditating in daily life. These include: that regular sitting practice will itself naturally help me to 'feel out' what meditating in daily life needs without my striving or agonising (if I am willing); that I am meditating in daily life unless I notice that I am not (and when I notice I'm not it is sufficient just to make the effort to 'come back'); that I can give others the benefit of the doubt unless they show me otherwise.

Supporting practice

Some other practical aspects which encourage my practice include:

- Remembering that training includes the informal: sitting in a chair relaxed and gently focused; taking a quiet walk in trees, countryside or along the street; reading a book which encourages me to practise. There is a world of difference between pretending to be informal through laziness, and following similar activities when our sense is that, at that moment, those activities would be creative ways to encourage our practice.

- Sitting with others when we can manage it — for example, going to a local meditation group or temple. When we are struggling, we find others are enthusiastic; at other times things are reversed. We experience the quiet dignity of people. We help. For everyone there are times of great enthusiasm in training and times of great difficulty. Training with others[3] can be a very helpful way to reground us and to bring us to balance more quickly within the lows and the highs.

- Talking with someone who we trust, and who has experience of meditation practice. This could be ringing a monk for spiritual counselling or chatting with someone at the meditation group. I have found it very helpful in my own practice to keep contact with a monk once I have got over the initial awkwardness of speaking on the phone. Though asking seriously, I have found it unhelpful to make my idea of spiritual counselling too lofty, or to judge whether I have a good enough question (or sometimes even a clearly formulated question at all). A judging attitude can act like salt on a snail, shrivelling it into its shell, and helps no-one.

- Listening to the wide range of downloadable Dharma talks from the various OBC temple websites, or subscribing to this Journal[4] or reading some of its articles online, all of which reflect the experience of those practising this style of meditation.

- Going on a retreat from time to time. I have found for myself that, gradually, there has been a movement from a view that the monastery or temple is the place where we do real practice, to appreciating that wherever we are, right now, is actually where we do real practice. Retreats then are a way of stepping out for a while from our normal routine, and later stepping back in, re-invigorated and inspired to practice more deeply: they provide an all-round environment where our practice is nourished, embraced and supported.

Not over-monitoring

Meditative awareness and our capacity to analyse and evaluate can be complementary to each other when used appropriately. But it can really stifle things if we keep monitoring and judging how we are progressing, and whether we are meditating properly or not. An 'answer' to this seems more to come through our deepening trust and conviction in meditative awareness and the process of meditation. Such trust and conviction arises from our willingness to practise and to persevere. It seems we need a working basis of trust to find a natural and deep trust that is already here.

I find it helpful to view 'coming back' (gently) as an integral aspect of meditation itself rather than as a 'hauling back' from not meditating to meditating, with all the negative judgements that the latter implies. We learn to trust that the meditative process continues whether we see this or not. Perseverance seems more important than self-judgement or cleverness.

Particularly when we meditate at home, many of us may have a sneaking suspicion that everyone else meditates better than we do (but this can't be true when you think about it). A few people may think that they meditate better than others (many of them may have a real problem!). It is a mistake to think that good meditation means always having a blank, 'peaceful' mind and bad meditation means its opposite. Thinking in this way makes us feel needlessly unhappy and probably like giving up. On busy days we will feel sleepy sometimes when we meditate in the evenings. On days involving much intellectual work there will be thoughts swirling through. On family crisis days there will be emotions arising when we sit. This is life. Such things need not get in the way of meditation, which has more the flavour of being present to whatever comes, without obstructing or clinging. And, even as we get distracted or caught up, we can right then notice the 'gluey' quality of following trains of thought or in getting caught up in streams of emotions. We learn gradually to be content just to 'come back', and that being still and present is not the same as having a blank mind.

We can't ever be someone else. When we truly start to understand this (which is quite sobering) we find that to be truly ourselves is something to be honoured and appreciated, rather than denigrated or 'puffed up'. We learn from others and, equally, we need to feel out compassionately how to practise with our own body and mind in our life situation as it is. Only we can make the contribution we are called to make. This is humbling and wonderful.

Notes

1. Great Master Dogen, in his search for a true master, conveys to us that he learnt so very much about the depth and profundity of meditation from observing the everyday activities of old monks in their daily functioning as the chief cooks of monasteries — see, for example, *Zen is Eternal Life*, Rev. Master P.T.N.H. Jiyu-Kennett, 4th Edition, (Mt. Shasta: Shasta Abbey Press, 1999) pp 152–154.

2. There are very helpful and comprehensive discussions of meditating in activity and daily life in this book and also in the chapter on 'The Life of Practice' in *Sitting Buddha*, Rev. Master Daishin Morgan, (Throssel Hole Press, 2004), pp 41–49.

3. OBC temples and affiliated meditation groups worldwide are shown on www.obcon.org/temps.html. There may also be newer meditation groups in formation which are not on this list, so it may be worth your contacting your nearest temple for further information if none of these are close to you.

4. For example there is a range of talks given by monks of the Order on http://obcon.org/dharma/audio-dharma-talks-2/, from Shasta Abbey in North America on http://www.shastaabbey.org/teachings.html, from Throssel Hole Buddhist Abbey in Europe on www.throssel.org.uk/dharma-talks, and on other temples' websites on www.obcon.org/temps.html, and articles are written by both monks and lay trainees in *The Journal of the Order of Buddhist Contemplatives*, some of which can be accessed online, on www.obcjournal.org.

Applying Meditation to Everyday Life

Rev. Master Jisho Perry

T he most common concept of education is that we learn from external stimuli—from books, lectures, art, music, TV, etc. There is another dimension to education; it comes from the literal meaning of the Latin which is to lead forth or draw out. This concept of education is to bring out that which is already there but not developed or fully understood. Socrates demonstrated the existence of past lives by showing that an uneducated slave boy already knew and understood profound mathematical truths by simply asking the boy questions and allowing him the opportunity of making the mental connections from the facts elicited. Although all of us have access to the Treasure House within us, we are not taught how to get at it. Putting meditation into practice is the process of learning how to be still within so that we can respond to the Buddha Nature within us. Out of the practice of serene reflection meditation arises the ability to be alert and sufficiently still in all activities so that we can fully use the capabilities we have. This does not make us gods or supermen; we still have the limitations of our humanity, but within those limitations there is another dimension which gradually opens up as the layers of ignorance are removed by spiritual training. Out of the ignorance we come to understanding: the alertness of meditation allows us to see the ignorance, the stillness allows us to plummet to its depths, and from there the understanding arises naturally when the selfish self is out of the way.

The underlying assumption here is that we are all part of the Cosmic Buddha and have the ability to be in contact with the Buddha Nature within us. This is the act of faith. When we act on faith we have the ability to be in touch with this adequacy or wholeness. To learn from anything, however, we must admit that there is something we do not know or do not understand. This creates an attitude of humility from which it is possible to accept knowledge and information. Both the willingness to admit that there is something we can learn and the acceptance of our own adequacy to learn it are essential. As Great Master Dogen puts it:

> When we wish to teach and enlighten all things by our-
> selves, we are deluded; when all things teach and enlight-
> en us, we are enlightened....[1]

We normally face the unknown with fear and inadequacy, which makes it very difficult to make the best choices or the most intelligent decisions. When this passes and we look through the eyes of humility from the knowledge of our own adequacy, which is no different from the willingness to grow and learn, then we can use the information—even the information of our own fears and inadequacies—effectively. This is when we actually learn something.

All this may seem somewhat irrelevant to the application of meditation to everyday life but, in fact, it is the very process of meditation, the sitting still within ourselves, that puts us in contact with both our own adequacy and our own humility. This opens the door to learn from everything. As we learn and grow we come to know that "the Light of Buddha is increasing in brilliance and the Wheel of the Dharma is always turning."[2]

Clarity arises naturally out of the effort of awareness. To pay attention is to stop putting our own ideas and opinions on the situation, simply and clearly to see things as they are. This is not a constant state. Clarity will arise and go as the sun arises and sets or goes behind a cloud only to reappear again. The more we make the effort, the more we see where that effort can be made. Each time we go through one door, the next one appears in the distance. Each time we see what there is to do, we also see how much we have not done. This need not be a source of discouragement or despair: it is doing the best we can when we see where we can do better and make the effort to do it. This is the "always going on, always becoming Buddha" of *The Scripture of Great Wisdom*.

Every day the koan[3] arises and we have the opportunity to put meditation into practice. We need to push back the frustration line or not react to the anger button or not tense up the greed tentacle, if only just for a little longer than usual. If we can give a bit more energy to the situation before we act on the anger, wait just a little longer before giving in to the frustration or acting on the greed, then stillness deepens and often we find that the frustration, anger or greed disappears. Sometimes we act on the anger or the frustration; then the only way to put meditation into action is simply to accept the situation and the consequences that develop. There is no need to complicate the situation with judgments or with guilt.

The area of greatest difficulty in daily life is not necessarily mechanical tasks or competence in work or even the complications of our relationships with others, but it is the relationship we have with ourselves and our greater self, the Selfless Self or the Buddha Nature. It is often easier to see when greed, hate or opinions get in the way of others than it is to see it in ourselves and often harder to know what to do with it when we do see it. But whatever the external situation, the only thing that we really have to deal with is ourselves, and the basic rules for dealing with ourselves and others are set out simply in the Precepts.[4] External situations and what others do are not as important as how we respond to them. The Buddha rejects nothing and uses everything to teach and enlighten us. Beneath the surface tensions or distrust or ambition, greed or anger, guilt or fear, lies something deeper—a stillness that is undisturbed by the superficial waves. When we act from this place something within us responds and it also responds in those with whom we relate: Buddha recognizes Buddha. It still takes a great deal of effort, energy and compassionate awareness, i.e., meditation, to do this and to do it effectively. "Forget the selfish self for a little and allow the mind to remain natural for this is very close to the Mind that seeks the Way."[5]

Meditation must be done daily and in all facets of our lives. This meditation is the forgetting of the selfish self, not holding on to being hurt or angry, proud, friendly, compassionate, self-righteous, fearful, adequate or inadequate. Let all these things arise and let them go without clinging to or suppressing any of them. This is not an easy task because we have learned through many lifetimes to act on these manifestations of the self. If we want to truly go deeper and know the Cosmic Buddha for ourselves then we have no choice but to willingly give up our clinging to all selfish forms. These forms that currently bind us, however, are the source of our freedom. They are as a door which, while we cling to our suffering, remains closed; yet in our willingness to embrace and accept this selfish self, the door opens to genuine selflessness and a personal knowledge of something bigger and more wonderful than anything we can imagine or dream about. Buddhism does not require that we get rid of the selfish self, only that we do not indulge or suppress it. Out of that continual effort, the selfishness is converted into the Buddha Nature. Our realization of It will come and go and in the comings and the returnings our relationship to It will change, as will our relationships to all things both animate and inanimate.

When we chop onions we may have tears in our eyes and this may temporarily cloud our vision; we still have the responsibility to waste neither time nor the onion, nor chop our finger. Putting meditation into practice is just this. It requires being still within as we chop the onion. To get caught by the fear of possibly chopping our fingers or, through lack of awareness, to cut ourselves is to fall out of the stillness. Stop. Follow the breath up the spine as you inhale and down the sternum as you exhale and continue with the onion or go and bandage the finger. Do what needs to be done. Whether it is dealing with sickness or death, driving a car or simply wiping the dust from the table, it requires the same quality of meditation— awareness and a willingness to do better. We cannot clean the table effectively unless we can see where it is dirty; and so within ourselves we have to see where the dust of fears, greeds, angers, guilts, opinions, etc., have knocked us out of that fundamentally still place and know that this very dust contains all of the Buddha Nature and is not for one moment separate or apart from it.

Intellectual work also needs the application of meditation. To sift through the morass of information we have been fed and to allow what is relevant and useful to manifest itself naturally is to put meditation into practice. This same effort must also be used in working through misunderstandings and figuring out what it is that we and others have not understood. It is easy to get ourselves worked up over these misunderstandings or to ignore important points that need explanation. As meditation deepens, something nags at us not to ignore misunderstandings or to get bothered by them; just patiently persist when the opportunity arises. Learning to meditate will not make everything simple, easy, effortless, uncomplicated and efficient. Reality is bigger than that; life is more complex.

There is a persistent myth that meditation will make you a superman. On a spiritual level it will put you in touch with the certain knowledge that there is Something In-destructible, the Unborn and Undying, and that it is possible to be in contact with this limitless energy. However, It is not available for selfish use unless you want to create a hell for yourself. It is subject to the Laws of the Universe,[6] which include the Precepts. It is available through gratitude and respect. All this naturally unfolds through meditation and its application. However, no matter how far one goes in meditation, one still remains human; there are physical limitations, emotions, thoughts, feelings, times of difficulty and times of stress. One continually comes around again to the beginning, standing there naked and unashamed before the Lord of the House, and out of the ignorance and the willingness to "sit up straight in the presence of the Buddha,"[7] compassion, love and wisdom have already manifested themselves. To be completely human is itself the manifestation of the Buddha Nature. This is realized by putting meditation into practice. Out of that place of stillness, the Buddha Himself participates in both the suffering and the joy and is completely unmoved by either.

Notes

1. Great Master Dogen, "Genjo-koan" ("The Problem of Everyday Life"), in *Zen is Eternal Life*, 3rd ed. rev., by Roshi P.T.N.H. Jiyu-Kennett (Mt. Shasta, California: Shasta Abbey Press, 1987), p. 172.
2. See *The Liturgy of the Order of Buddhist Contemplatives for the Laity,* comp. Rev. Master P.T.N.H. Jiyu-Kennett, M.O.B.C., 2nd ed. rev. (Mt. Shasta, California: Shasta Abbey Press, 1990), p. 112.

3. Any spiritual problem or obstacle we think separates us from the Eternal.

4. For the Buddhist Precepts, see pp. 50–66 in this book.

5. Dogen, "Gyakudo-yojinshu" ("Important Aspects of Zazen"), in *Zen is Eternal Life,* by Jiyu-Kennett, p. 126.

6. The Five Laws of the Universe:

The physical world is not answerable to my personal will.

The Law of Change.

The Law of Karma is inevitable and inexorable.

Without fail evil is vanquished and good prevails; this too is inexorable.

The intuitive knowledge of Buddha Nature occurs to all men.

7. Dogen, "Shushogi" ("Training and Enlightenment"), in *Zen is Eternal Life*, by Jiyu-Kennett, p. 157.

9 780930 066284